The Essential Second Amendment Guide

WAYNE LaPIERRE
Executive Vice President
National Rifle Association of America

BORU BOOKS

Bor

The Essential Second Amendment Guide

Additional information available from:
National Rifle Association of America
11250 Waples Mill Road
Fairfax, VA 22030
1-800-672-3888
www.NRA.org

Cover Painting:
"Stand Your Ground - Battle of Lexington Green"
by Don Troiani
www.historicalimagebank.com

Published in the United States by
Boru Publishing, Inc.
11250 Waples Mill Road Third Floor
Fairfax, VA 22030

ISBN: 978-0-9724131-1-4

Table of Contents

Preface

Why I Wrote This Book For You

Dear Fellow American,

The Second Amendment of the Bill of Rights guarantees your right to keep and bear arms.

You have a right to own a gun for defense of family and home. You have a right to own a gun for hunting, shooting or collecting. You have the right to own a gun to break the chains of tyranny.

Our Founding Fathers said it. Our Constitution guarantees it. Our courts affirm it. Our laws protect it.

Yet there are politicians, bureaucrats and members of the media elite who want to trample our freedoms. They say you can't be trusted to own a firearm. They say your freedoms are the cause of crime. They say that the government has the right to determine whether you *need* to own a gun. They say there is no human right to self-defense.

They portray law-abiding gun owners like you as the members of some lunatic fringe. They attack you in the press and call you a second-class citizen. They say your faith in firearm freedom has no place in today's world. They want to muzzle and marginalize you, and strip you of your political power.

Because you stand in the way of their vision of a firearm-free America, where the Second Amendment ceases to exist and our Constitution is null and void.

I have a different vision.

In the Second Amendment, we have the purest and most precious form of freedom because it is the one freedom that gives common men and women uncommon power to defend all freedoms.

For thirty years, I have dedicated my life to the defense of our Second Amendment rights. In the halls of Congress, on the plaintiff's bench and under the klieg lights of media inquisition, I have stood toe to toe with our enemies. I have answered every lie, exposed every deception and countered every trick and tactic.

In this book, I am giving you the battle-tested arguments—and an arsenal of facts, figures and anecdotes—that I use every day. My hope is that you'll carry this book with you, read it again and again, and share its truths with all who will listen.

Whether you're standing at your back fence arguing with a neighbor, confronting a politician or firing off a letter to the editor of your local paper, build your arguments on the bedrock foundation of this book. On its pages you will find the words that, after thirty years, have not yielded an inch of ground to the anti-gunners.

Please keep this book as your constant companion, and use it to make your voice heard and your vote count. Because in the end, your commitment to our cause is all that guarantees that the Second Amendment survives and thrives for generations to come.

Thank you for keeping the flame of freedom burning brightly in American hearts.

Yours in Freedom,

Wayne LaPierre, September, 2007

6

Introduction

The Second Amendment guarantees: "A well regulated Militia, being necessary to the security of a free State, the right of the people to keep and bear Arms, shall not be infringed."

This guarantees a citizen's right to keep and bear arms for personal and community defense. The Founders trusted an armed citizenry as the best safeguard against the possibility of a tyrannical government, and the armed citizens would also be able to exercise the natural right to defend their homes.

The Founders distrusted a government that wouldn't trust its people. To fulfill the promise of the Declaration of Independence, the authors of the U.S. Constitution and its Bill of Rights made it clear that individual rights were paramount. The Bill of Rights, wrote James Madison, was "calculated to secure the personal rights of the people."

In 1776, America's Founders came together in Philadelphia to draw up a "Declaration of Independence," ending political ties to Great Britain. Written by Thomas Jefferson, it is the fundamental statement of people's rights, and the source of the government's powers:

> *WE hold these Truths to be self-evident, that all Men are created equal, that they are endowed by their Creator with certain unalienable Rights, that among these are Life, Liberty, and the Pursuit of Happiness— That to secure these Rights, Governments are instituted among Men, deriving their just Powers from the Consent of the Governed.*

The Founders were declaring that we are all equal, and that we are defined by rights that we are born with, not those given to us by government. Among those rights is the right to pursue happiness–to live our lives as we think best, as long as we respect the right of all other individuals to do the same. The Founders also declared that governments are created by people to secure their rights. Whatever powers government has are not "just" unless they come from us, the people.

Eleven years later, after the war for independence had been won, our Founders assembled once again to draw up a plan for governing the new nation. That plan would be ratified two years later as the Constitution of the United States of America.

To understand the true meaning of the Second Amendment, it is important to understand the men who wrote and ratified it, and the issues they faced in creating the Constitution. During the debate over the ratification of the Constitution, there was significant concern that a strong federal government would trample on the individual rights of citizens–as had happened under British rule.

To protect the basic rights of Americans—rights which each person possesses and that are guaranteed, but not granted, by any government—the framers added the first ten amendments to the Constitution as a package. Those amendments have come to be known as the Bill of Rights. They represent the fundamental freedoms that are at the heart of our society, including freedom of speech, freedom of religion and the right of the people to keep and bear arms.

The History of Our Rights

The British people did not have a written constitution as we have in the United States. However, they did have a tradition of protecting individual rights from government. Those rights were set forth in a number of documents, including the Magna Carta and the English Declaration of Rights. The Founders who wrote the Bill of Rights drew many of their ideas from the traditions of English "common law," which is the body of legal tradition and court decisions that acted as an unwritten constitution and as a balance to the power of English kings.

The Founders believed in the basic rights of "the people" as described in those documents and in the common law. One of these rights was the right of the common people to bear arms, which was specifically recognized in the English Declaration of Rights of 1689.

The Founders also recognized that without a blueprint for what powers government could exercise, the rights of the people would always be subject to being violated. The Constitution, and particularly the Bill of Rights, was created to specifically describe the powers of government and the rights of individuals government was not allowed to infringe.

Today, some claim that banning only certain firearms does not constitute an infringement of Second Amendment rights. That ploy is not new. George Mason exposed it at Virginia's Constitutional Convention in 1788: "[W]hen the resolution of enslaving America was formed in Great Britain, the British Parliament was advised by an artful man . . . to disarm the people; that it was the best and most effectual way to enslave them; but that they should not do it openly, but weaken them, and let them sink gradually."

Our founders risked their lives to create a free nation, and they guaranteed freedom as the birthright of American citizens through the Bill of Rights. The Second Amendment remains the first right among equals, because it is the one we turn to when all else fails.

James Madison, author of the Second Amendment, wrote that Americans had "the advantage of being armed," that was lacking in other nations, where "the governments are afraid to trust the people with arms." Patrick Henry proclaimed the "great object is that every man be armed. . . . Everyone who is able may have a gun." The Second Amendment was then, as it is today, about freedom and the means to protect it.

Chapter 1:
The Founders' Intent

"[The NRA] should either put up or admit there is no Second Amendment guarantee.... We are confident in our challenge because there is no confusion in the law on this issue."

-R. William Ide III, President American Bar Association, April 15, 1994

A common claim of the anti-gun lobby is that our nation's Founders never meant that individuals should be armed; they only intended for the Second Amendment to apply to a militia, such as the National Guard.

These self-proclaimed interpreters of the Constitution also ignore the Second Amendment's specific reference to "the right of the people." The fact that "rights of the people" appear in the First, Fourth, Ninth, and Tenth Amendments as well—and that the courts have ruled repeatedly that these rights belong to individuals, not to governments—matters little to them. They retreat to their standard charge that the Founders never intended for the people to have the right to keep and bear arms.

Even a casual reading of our Founders' works would prove these foes of the Second Amendment wrong. Volumes upon volumes of articles, pamphlets, speeches, and documents that laid the foundation for the Bill of Rights clearly define the Founders' purpose, including what they intended with the Second Amendment.

In pre-revolution America, the threats posed by a standing British army loomed large in the minds of the colonists. Resistance was widespread. In response to the dissent, the British increased their military presence. Two years later, in 1770, unarmed citizens were gunned down in the streets of Boston, in what became known as the Boston Massacre.

The Boston Massacre was the fuse that lit the powder keg of debate over the right of the people to be armed. Ironically enough, the colonists did in fact have the right to be armed under English common law. John Adams, then serving as a defense counsel for one of the British soldiers who participated in the shooting, acknowledged this in his opening argument:

Here, every private person is authorized to arm himself, and on the strength of this authority, I do not deny the inhabitants had a right to arm themselves at that time, for their defense, not for offense....

With the courts of the time affirming the colonists' right to keep and bear arms, the British oppressors were placed between the proverbial "rock and a hard place." From that point on, quelling dissent would involve the denial of a basic right afforded all British citizens.

Nonetheless, the British proceeded down a path that could only lead to revolution. Not only did the British strengthen their military chokehold on Boston, they instituted a program of arms confiscation. Citizens could leave the city only upon "depositing their arms with their own magistrates."

British confiscation of arms focused the attention of our Founders on the threats posed by a standing army quartered among the people, and the necessity of having an armed citizenry to prevent the tyranny of such an occupying force.

No doubt inspired by the Boston arms confiscations, George Mason, the subsequent co-author of the Second Amendment, wrote in his Fairfax County Militia Plan:

> *[A] well-regulated Militia, composed of the Gentlemen, Freeholders, and other Freemen was necessary to protect our ancient laws and liberty from the standing army. ... And we do each of us, for ourselves respectively, promise and engage to keep a good Fire-lock in proper order & to furnish Ourselves as soon as possible with, & always keep by us, one Pound of Gunpowder, four Pounds of Lead, one Dozen Gun Flints, and a pair of Bullet Moulds, with a Cartouch Box, or powder horn, and Bag for Balls.*

The anti-gun lobby devotes considerable intellectual energy to the definition of "militia" as it appears in Mason's writings. Mason, however, made a very clear distinction between a "standing army," such as a guard unit, and a "militia," composed of private citizens. The anti-gunners nevertheless claim that the militia refers to a national guard, not to the citizenry at large. To eliminate any doubt, however, Mason made his point clear in other writings as, for example, when he said, "To disarm the people [is] the best and most effectual way to enslave them."

Mason's sentiments were echoed by Samuel Adams who admonished the uneasy colonists that:

> *[I]t is always dangerous to the liberties of the people to have an army stationed among them, over which*

*they have no control.... The Militia is composed of
free Citizens. There is therefore no Danger of their
making use of their power to the destruction of their
own Rights, or suffering others to invade them.*

In this passage, Adams further clarified Mason's
thinking on the power of government with respect to the
armed citizen: rights are sacred when the beneficiaries of
those rights are entrusted with their safekeeping, and have
the means to do so.

Our Founders clearly understood that, once armed,
Americans would defend their freedoms to the last breath.
Nowhere was this notion more evident than in Patrick
Henry's "Give me liberty, or give me death" speech.
The context of that oration-the importance of an armed
population-has unfortunately been lost in today's
"politically correct" anti-gun climate. Yet, Henry's words
are there to defend the embattled Second Amendment.
When speaking of revolution, Henry proclaimed:

*They tell us...that we are weak-unable to cope with
so formidable an adversary. But when shall we be
stronger? ...Will it be when we are totally disarmed,
and when a British guard shall be stationed in every
house? ... Three million people, armed in the holy
cause of liberty... are invincible by any force which
our enemy can send against us.*

Patrick Henry not only issued this warning, he acted
upon it. Following the British attempt to seize arms and
ammunition in Boston, and the subsequent historic
skirmish at Lexington, the British seized gunpowder at

Williamsburg, Virginia. The Hanover Independent Militia, led by Henry himself, was unable to retake the powder, but they forced the British to pay restitution. At this point, the British denial of the colonists' right to keep and bear arms became the driving force behind the armed resistance.

This fundamental right-the importance of an American's ability to defend his liberties-became the principal argument of our Founders for independence. Following the "shot heard round the world" at Lexington, Thomas Jefferson penned these words in the Virginia Constitution of 1776: "[N]o free man shall be debarred the use of arms within his own land."

Nowhere are Jefferson's thoughts about the rights and powers of the citizenry more explicit than in the Declaration of Independence: "Governments are instituted among Men, deriving their just powers from the consent of the governed. That whenever any form of Government becomes destructive of these ends, it is the Right of the People to alter or abolish it."

Certainly Jefferson, and his co-authors of the Declaration, preferred peaceful changes in government. But those four words-"the Right of the People"-state in plain language that the people have the right, must have the right, to take whatever measures necessary, including force, to abolish oppressive government.

Jefferson was not alone in sounding the call to arms. Henry, Adams, Washington all called upon the colonists to arm themselves. And the call was issued to all Americans, not only landowners and freemen. Thomas Paine, renowned for his treatise, *Common Sense*, urged religious pacifists to take up arms in his pamphlet "Thoughts on Defensive War:"

*[T]he balance of power is the scale of peace. The
same balance would be preserved were all the world
not destitute of arms, for all would be alike; but
since some will not, others dare not lay them aside....
Horrid mischief would ensue were one half the world
deprived of the use of them ... the weak will become a
prey to the strong.*

In the case of the American Revolution, however, it
was the strong who became the prey of the weak. Indeed,
seasoned British troops were beleaguered by the armed
and resolute citizens of the colonies.

Our Founders wasted no time in attributing this
victory to the right of the people to keep and bear arms.
James Madison, the father of the Second Amendment,
congratulated his countrymen:

Americans [have] the right and advantage of
being armed-unlike citizens of other countries whose
governments are afraid to trust the people with arms.

Indeed, it was President George Washington who
urged the first Congress to pass an act enrolling the entire
adult male citizenry in a general militia. The father of our
country further urged that "A free people ought not only to
be armed, but disciplined."

Washington's sentiments about the militia, and who
should be included in the militia in the infant United
States, were echoed by George Mason in the debate on
the ratification of the Constitution before the Virginia
Assembly: "I ask, sir, what is the militia? It is the whole
people, except for a few public officials."

"Except for a few public officials." With these six
words, George Mason made explicit his deep-set belief

that the individual armed citizen was the key to protection against government excesses and in defense of freedom.

James Madison expanded on this point in *The Federalist* No. 46, where he downplayed the threat of seizure of authority by a federal army, because such a move would be opposed by "a militia amounting to half a million men."

In 1790, since the population of the United States was about 800,000, Madison wasn't referring to state reserves. By militia, Madison obviously meant every able-bodied man capable of bearing arms. This, undoubtedly, was also the meaning of "militia" when the Second Amendment was written.

Across the nation, Federalists echoed our Founders' insistence that the right to keep and bear arms become part of the Constitution. In a pamphlet advocating Pennsylvania's ratification of the Constitution, patriot and statesman Noah Webster declared:

> *Before a standing army can rule, the people must be disarmed; as they are in almost every kingdom in Europe. The supreme power in America cannot enforce unjust laws by the sword, because the whole body of the people are armed, and constitute a force superior to any band of regular troops that can be, on any pretense, raised in the United States.*

Not only did our Founders focus their debate on the right of the people to keep and bear arms, they devoted considerable energy to issuing a warning to future generations that the battle to defend these freedoms will take precedence over all other work.

It was Patrick Henry at the Virginia convention on the ratification of the Constitution who articulated the necessity of guarding the rights of an armed citizenry:

> *Guard with jealous attention the public liberty. Suspect every one who approaches that jewel. Unfortunately, nothing will preserve it but downright force. Whenever you give up that force, you are ruined.*

And James Madison, in the *National Gazette*, January 19, 1792:

> *Liberty and order will never be perfectly safe until a trespass on the Constitutional provisions for either, shall be felt with the same keenness that resents an invasion of the dearest rights.*

Unfortunately, the invasion of our dearest rights is taking place today. There are dozens of anti-gun bills before the United States Congress, and hundreds more before the state legislatures and city councils. Anti-gun politicians, in the name of fighting crime or terrorism, are attacking the sacred constitutional rights of law-abiding American citizens. Today, it is politically correct to ignore the Founders and their clear intent. For the sake of political expediency, the anti-gun lobby and politicians, and their media allies, have twisted, tangled, and reinterpreted the Founders' words. The anti-gunners would do well to pay heed to the words of Benjamin Franklin:

> *They that can give up essential liberty to purchase a little temporary safety, deserve neither liberty nor safety.*

Unfortunately, a large part of this tragedy-the wanton disregard of our essential liberties-can be laid at the feet of Americans who have not taken action to protect their freedoms. To quote C.S. Lewis: "We laugh at honor and are shocked to find traitors in our midst."

Every American must leap to the defense of his or her liberties. We must answer, word for word, the false and vicious attacks that pour out from the TV screen and newspaper pages around the country. We must attend town meetings in protest and we must hold our elected officials accountable. We must not allow them to misinterpret our Founders' directives. Then, and only then, will freedom be safe for future generations.

In the words of Dwight D. Eisenhower:

Freedom has its life in the hearts, the actions, the spirit of men and so it must be daily earned and refreshed-else like a flower cut from its life-giving roots, it will wither and die.

Chapter 2:
"The Right Of The People To Keep And Bear Arms"

Columnist Don Shoemaker dismisses as "idiocy" the belief that the Second Amendment prevents government from banning guns.

Leonard Larsen of Scripps-Howard News Service says "only gun nut simpletons [and] NRA propagandists... defend against gun controls on constitutional grounds."

Such tirades, including the suggestion that the constitutional right keep and bear arms applies only to the states' militia and National Guard, are typical of media endorsement of anti-gun propaganda.

Some columnists are willing to concede, however, that their Second Amendment philosophy doesn't square with scholarship on the issue. In a 1991 column in the *Washington Post*, after reading Sanford Levinson's *Yale Law Journal* article, "The Embarrassing Second Amendment," George F. Will wrote:

The National Rifle Association is perhaps correct and certainly is plausible in its `strong' reading of the Second Amendment protection of private gun ownership. Therefore gun control advocates who want to square their policy preferences with the Constitution should squarely face the need to deconstitutionalize the subject by repealing the embarrassing [Second] amendment."

Anti-gun lawyer-activist, Michael Kinsley, then co-host on CNN's "Crossfire" and formerly editor-in-chief of the *New Republic*, regularly calls for gun control and proudly held membership in Handgun Control, Inc. (now known as The Brady Campaign). However, in a 1990 op-ed article in the *Washington Post*, Kinsley wrote:

> *Unfortunately, there is the Second Amendment to the Constitution.*
>
> *The purpose of the First Amendment's free-speech guarantee was pretty clearly to protect political discourse. But liberals reject the notion that free speech is therefore limited to political topics, even broadly defined. True, that purpose is not inscribed in the amendment itself. But why leap to the conclusion that a broadly worded constitutional freedom ("the right of the people to keep and bear arms") is narrowly limited by its stated purpose, unless you're trying to explain it away? My New Republic colleague Mickey Kaus says that if liberals interpreted the Second Amendment the way they interpret the rest of the Bill of Rights, there would be law professors arguing that gun ownership is mandatory.*

Despite an occasional admission that the Second Amendment means what it says, many columnists, with little or no understanding of the roots of the Constitution, rush to embrace a view that finds virtually no support in the academic community among high-ranking constitutional rights scholars. That's not opinion, that's plain truth.

The vast majority of Second Amendment scholars

support the individual rights view. The numbers are overwhelming: since 1980, nearly 90 law review articles have endorsed the individual rights interpretation. That's more than three times the number of post-1980 articles supporting the "collective rights" view—and ten of those grew out of a single symposium to which no individual rights supporters were invited.

The individual rights authors include leading constitutional scholars who don't own guns and who "never expected or desired the evidence to crush the anti-gun position."

Take Duke Law School's William Van Alstyne, a former American Civil Liberties Union (ACLU) national board member, who has been twice selected in polls of judges, attorneys and law professors as an outstanding prospect for appointment to the Supreme Court. Professor Van Alstyne writes that people who are serious about civil liberties "begin with a constitutional understanding that declines to trivialize the Second Amendment, just as they decline likewise to trivialize any other right guaranteed to the people by the Constitution."

Professor Van Alstyne also says unflinchingly:

> *Nor is the NRA to be faulted for taking the Second Amendment seriously when others tend now to look away. Its stance here is no more and no less than one might take equally in response to proposed regulations of any other matter enumerated in the Bill of Rights, whether it affects one's freedom of speech or, as here, the right to keep and bear arms.*

Professor Sanford Levinson of the University of Texas Law School, co-author of a standard law school text on the Constitution, is another ACLU stalwart. In his 1989 *Yale Law Journal* article, cited by George Will, Professor Levinson candidly admits his own embarrassment at concluding that private gun ownership *cannot* be prohibited—his embarrassment apparently stemming from a belief that his research could find the opposite.

Levinson and Yale Law Professor Akhil Amar, a Professor of Constitutional Law at Yale University, enjoy stature among liberal constitutional scholars. Yet Amar trounces the anti-gun states' right theory almost savagely, reiterating over and over again that the Second Amendment guarantees the right to arms to "the people", not "the states":

> *[W]hen the Constitution means "states" it says so.... The ultimate right to keep and bear arms belongs to "the people," not the "states."... Thus the "people" at the core of the Second Amendment [are] the same "We the People" who "ordain and establish" the Constitution and whose right to assemble ... [is] at the core of the First Amendment.... Nowadays, it is quite common to speak loosely of the National Guard as "the state militia," but [when the Second Amendment was written]... "the militia" referred to all Citizens capable of bearing arms. [So] "the militia" is identical to "the people" ...."*

Are these eminent constitutional scholars "gun nut simpletons, [and] NRA propagandists"? Michael Kinsley doesn't think so.

After reviewing a *Michigan Law Review* article by Professor Don Kates, Kinsley wrote in an op-ed in the

Washington Post:

> *If there is a reply, the [gun] controllers haven't made it... Establishing that a flat ban on handguns would be [unconstitutional,] Kates builds a distressingly good case.*

Kinsley is distressed because "a flat ban on handguns," preferably all guns, is precisely what he wants. His article concludes:

> *Gun nuts are unconvincing (at least to me) in their attempts to argue that the individual right to bear arms is still as vital to freedom as it was in 1792. But the right is still there.*

Two other major contributors to constitutional scholarship are neutral historians. One is Professor Joyce Lee Malcolm, a political historian whose work on the English and American origins of the right to arms has been underwritten by the American Bar Foundation, Harvard Law School and the National Endowment for the Humanities. In *To Keep And Bear Arms: The Origins of An Anglo-American Right*, Professor Malcolm writes:

> *The Second Amendment was meant to accomplish two distinct goals.... First, it was meant to guarantee the individual's right to have arms for self-defense and self-preservation... These privately owned arms were meant to serve a larger purpose [militia service] as well... and it is the coupling of these two objectives that has caused the most confusion. The customary American militia necessitated an armed public ...*

> *the militia [being] ... the body of the people.... The argument that today's National Guardsmen, members of a select militia, would constitute the only persons entitled to keep and bear arms has no historical foundation.*

Professor Robert Shalhope, a non-gun owning intellectual historian, whose interest is the philosophy of the Founders, agrees. Professor Shalhope writes, in a 1982 edition of the *Journal of American History*:

> *When James Madison and his colleagues drafted the Bill of Rights they ... firmly believed in two distinct principles: (1) Individuals had the right to possess arms to defend themselves and their property; and (2) states retained the right to maintain militias composed of these individually armed citizens.... Clearly, these men believed that the perpetuation of a republican spirit and character in their society depended upon the freeman's possession of arms as well as his ability and willingness to defend both himself and his society.*

As Professor Kates put it: "Historical research shows that our Founding Fathers out NRAed the NRA."

Thomas Paine believed it would be better for "all the world to lay [arms] aside ... and settle matters by negotiation: but unless the whole will, the matter ends, and I take up my musket and thank Heaven He has put it in my power."

Paine clearly doubted that criminals could be disarmed and deemed it important that decent people be armed against criminals:

The peaceable part of mankind will be continually overrun by the vile and abandoned while they neglect the means of self-defense.... [Weakness] allures the ruffian [, but] arms like laws discourage and keep the invader and plunderer in awe and preserve order in the world.... Horrid mischief would ensue were [the good] deprived of the use of them... the weak will become a prey to the strong.

Or, simply stated–criminals prefer unarmed victims. Consider the similar views of the great 18th Century Italian criminologist Cesare Beccaria, that could be described as a rendition of today's slogan "when guns are outlawed only outlaws will have guns."

Thomas Jefferson translated the following from Beccaria's Italian and laboriously copied it in long-hand into his own personal compilation of great quotations:

False is the idea of utility that sacrifices a thousand real advantages for one imaginary or trifling inconvenience; that would take fire from men because it burns, and water because one may drown in it; that has no remedy for evils, except destruction. The laws that forbid the carrying of arms are laws of such a nature. They disarm those only who are neither inclined nor determined to commit crimes. Can it be supposed that those who have the courage to violate the most sacred laws of humanity, the most important of the code, will respect the less important and arbitrary ones, which can be violated with ease and impunity, and which, if strictly obeyed, would put an end to personal liberty—so dear to men, so dear to the enlightened legislator—and subject innocent persons to all the vexations that the quality alone ought to suffer? Such laws make things worse for the assaulted and better for the assailants; they serve rather to encourage than to prevent homicides, for an unarmed man may be attacked with greater confidence than an armed man. They ought to be designated as laws not preventive but fearful of crimes, produced by the tumultuous impression of a few isolated facts, and not by thoughtful consideration of the inconveniences and advantages of a universal decree.

The Founders unanimously agreed. "The great object," thundered Anti-Federalist Patrick Henry, "is that every man be armed." James Madison, Federalist author of the Bill of Rights, reviled tyrants for being "afraid to trust the people with arms" and extolled "the advantage of being armed, which the Americans possess over the people of almost every other nation."

The Anti-Federalists endorsed Madison's Bill of Rights while claiming it was their own idea. They characterized the Second Amendment as a mere rewording of Sam Adams' proposal "that the ... Constitution be never construed to prevent the people who are peaceable citizens from keeping their own arms." The Federalist analysis said the Amendment confirmed to the people "their private arms."

Fortunately, the ideas of our nation's earliest leaders have not been forgotten by some of their counterparts today. In 2004, in response to a request from then-Attorney General John Ashcroft, the Department of Justice's Office of Legal Counsel delivered an exhaustive report on the meaning of the Second Amendment.

In that report, entitled "Whether the Second Amendment

Ensures an Individual Right," some of DOJ's top lawyers advised the Attorney General—and the world—that "[t]he Second Amendment secures a personal right of individuals, not a collective right that may only be invoked by a State or a quasi-collective right restricted to persons serving in organized militia units."

Exhaustively analyzing the Founders' writings in the light of modern scholarship, and parsing the meaning of their words and phrases they used, the memo details the evolution of the Second Amendment, from the state constitutional conventions to its ultimate adoption.

And—in keeping with the traditional rule that there's no right without a remedy to enforce it, the memo adds that "[i]ndividuals may bring claims or raise challenges based on a violation of their rights under the Second Amendment just as they do to vindicate individual rights secured by other provisions of the Bill of Rights."

In other words, the Second Amendment means what it says. It's a right of the people. Period.

Limitations On The Right To Arms

Are there any limits on either the kinds of arms the Second Amendment guarantees or the kinds of people it protects? Like other leading constitutional scholars, Professor Van Alstyne rejects the claim that the Second Amendment "does not extend to handguns ... [as] wholly inconsistent with any sensible understanding of a meaningful right to keep arms as a personal right."

But neither felons nor children under 18 years have the right to own arms any more than they have the right to vote. This is based on solid historical reasons analyzed in law reviews. For more than 70 years the NRA has supported laws to prohibit gun ownership by those who have been convicted of violent crime.

By the same token, NRA has for decades supported and helped pass tough penalties to keep those who misuse guns in prison where they belong.

For example, NRA was one of the earliest and strongest supporters of "Project Exile"—an intensive enforcement program that began in Richmond, Virginia, where it brought the full weight of federal prosecution to bear on convicted felons and violent criminals using guns. Before Project Exile began in 1997, the city of Richmond suffered the second highest per capita homicide rate in the nation. Project Exile saved lives. Homicides in 1999 were 46% below 1997 for the lowest number since 1987. Gun crimes declined an amazing 65%.

Yet, despite NRA support for tough law enforcement, anti-individual rights propagandists accuse NRA of claiming the Second Amendment guarantees guns for all (including criminals), and that it guarantees a right to own weapons like bazookas and bombs. Such has never been the case—and they know it.

The right to arms clearly protects ordinary small arms that citizens would bear in defense of life and liberty— handguns, rifles, and shotguns—including "assault weapons." In fact, "assault weapons" are just ordinary semi-automatic firearms like those which have existed in this country for about a century. They fire no faster than revolvers or pump action rifles and shotguns. As George Washington University law professor Robert Cottrol notes:

It has been argued that "assault weapons" are far more deadly than 18th Century arms. Actually, modern medical technology makes them far less deadly than blunderbusses were in the 18th Century. (In fact, "assault weapons" are less deadly—and far less often used in crime—than ordinary shotguns or hunting rifles.)

Professors Cottrol and Kates agree that if the many changes in conditions since 1792 when the Second Amendment was enacted could justify ignoring it, other rights protected by the Bill of Rights would also be endangered.

Take, for instance, radio, TV and the movies. These didn't exist when the Bill of Rights was written, yet all three are now embraced by its free speech and press clauses. The Supreme Court enforces that stand.

By the same token, sensationalized national network coverage results in new crimes. Car-jacking, first confined to Michigan, spread nationwide as other criminals picked up the idea. Other such detriments result from continuing to recognize freedom of the press in our modern era. Yet we must, and do, continue to expand our constitutional free press protections to cover new forms of communication as they multiply and expand.

Quoting Professors Cottrol and Kates:

If the Bill of Rights is to continue, we must apply its spirit even as conditions change. That is the nub of the Second Amendment controversy: Modern intellectuals who tend to feel self-defense is barbaric—that government should have a monopoly of arms with

*the people being dependent on it for protection—
have difficulty accepting the Founders' diametrically
opposite views.*

But as the Supreme Court said when its decisions
vindicating the privilege against self-incrimination were
assailed as inconsistent with government's need to detect
modern criminals and subversives:

*If it be thought that the privilege is outmoded in the
conditions of this modern age, then the thing to do
is to [amend] it out of the Constitution, not to whittle
it down by the subtle encroachments of judicial
opinion. Ullmann v. United States, 350 U.S. 422, 427-
28 (1956).*

Can An Armed People Resist Tyranny?

Claiming that the only purpose of the right to arms
is to enable citizens to resist a military takeover of our
government, gun ban activists sometimes argue that the
Second Amendment is obsolete since a populace armed
with only small arms cannot defeat a modern army. That
is doubly wrong. Even if overthrowing tyranny were the
Amendment's only purpose, the claim that an armed
populace cannot successfully resist stems from wantonly
misportraying the issue as whether people with handguns
can attack tanks.

The 20th Century provides no example of a determined
populace which had access to small arms being defeated by
a modern army. The Russians lost in Afghanistan and the

U.S. and French in Vietnam. In China and Cuba, Chiang Kai-shek and Batista lost; in Nicaragua so did both Somoza and the Sandinistas. Modern nations such as Algeria, Angola, Ireland, Israel, Mozambique, and Zimbabwe only exist because guerrilla warfare can triumph over modern armies.

While we may not approve all the governments that have resulted, each of these triumphs exemplifies a simple truth: a determined people who have the means to maintain prolonged war against a modern army can battle it to a standstill, subverting major portions of the army or defeating it themselves or with major arms supplied by outside forces.

The Founders' main purpose in guaranteeing the right to keep and bear arms was not only to overthrow tyrants. They saw the right to arms as a crucial element in what they believed to be the prime natural right—self-defense.

The claim that the right to arms is outmoded is held by opinion leaders who detest armed personal self-defense, which they view, in the words of Ramsey Clark, as "anarchy, not order under law—a jungle where each relies on himself for survival".

Or as the *Washington Post* editorializes: "The need that some homeowners and shopkeepers believe they have for weapons to defend themselves" represents "the worst instincts in the human character."

The Brady Campaign (formerly Handgun Control, Inc.) chairperson Sarah Brady claimed "the only reason for guns in civilian hands is for sporting purposes"—not self-defense. "Pete" Shields, Brady's predecessor as HCI head, advised in his book, *Guns Don't Die*, that victims never resist rape or robbery: "give them what they want or run".

To assure that people can't be armed to resist, Brady proposed a national licensing law with gun ownership confined to sportsmen — self-defense not being a proper ground for gun ownership ("A Little Control, A Lot of Guns", *New York Times*, Aug. 15, 1993, quoting Sarah Brady). In an October 22, 1993 editorial, the *Los Angeles Times* agreed.

But author Jeff Snyder points out in his essay -- "A Nation of Cowards" in *The Public Interest* (Fall 1993):

> *As the Founding Fathers knew well, a government that does not trust its honest, law-abiding, taxpaying citizens with the means of self-defense is not itself worthy of trust. Laws disarming honest citizens proclaim that the government is the master, not the servant of the people...*

> *The Bill of Rights does not grant rights to the people, such that its repeal would legitimately confer upon government the powers otherwise proscribed. The Bill of Rights is the list of the fundamental, inalienable rights, endowed in man by his Creator, that define what it means to be a free and independent people, the rights which must exist to ensure that government governs only with the consent of the people.*

Chapter 3: Congress and the Second Amendment: Views of the Popular Branch

Highly contentious opinions handed down by the judicial branch cause some Americans to lose sight of the fact that the legislative branch interprets the United States Constitution when it legislates, rendering its own interpretations of what the Constitution permits or does not allow. Indeed, Congress enacts laws intended to protect constitutional rights and, in rare instances, declares the nature of those rights.

Since it is elected (and hence held in check) by the people, Congress has never given any support for the newly minted argument that the Second Amendment fails to protect any right of the people, and instead ensures a nonsensical "collective right" of states to maintain militias. To the contrary, in the Constitution's vocabulary, states have powers, not rights, and federal–state powers regarding the militia are dealt with elsewhere in the Constitution.

On four occasions—in 1866, 1941, 1986, and 2005—Congress enacted statutes to reaffirm the Second Amendment's guarantee of personal freedom and to adopt specific safeguards to enforce it. And in 2006, Congress acted to protect the Second Amendment during disasters and other emergencies.

These statutory declarations by Congress have been the subject of little or no comment by the judiciary or legal historians. The first two were enacted at times of great historical crisis. The 1866 declaration was enacted to protect the rights of freed slaves to keep and bear arms following a tumultuous civil war and at the outset of the subsequent, chaotic Reconstruction period. The 1941 enactment was intended to reassure Americans that preparations for war would not include repressive or tyrannical policies against firearms owners, and it was passed shortly before the Japanese sneak attack on Pearl Harbor, which forced the United States into World War II.

Two more recent enactments sought to reverse outrageous excesses involving America's legal system. In 1986, Congress reacted to overzealous enforcement policies under the federal firearms law by passing reform legislation. In 2005, recognizing that the state and federal judicial systems were being misused in an attempt to destroy America's firearms industry, Congress stepped in to end this threat to the Second Amendment.

Finally, in 2006, Congress acted to prevent arbitrary government intrusions against the Second Amendment by government agencies during "states of emergency."

The hidden history of these five enactments of Congress makes absolutely clear that keeping and bearing arms is an individual right that may not be infringed by the government, whether federal or state.

The Freedmen's Bureau Act of 1866:
The Constitutional Right to Bear Arms

Like the rest of the Bill of Rights, the Second Amendment was originally viewed by the Supreme Court as guaranteeing individual rights against action by the federal government, but not against the states. At the end of the War Between the States, slavery was abolished; however, Southern states continued to treat black freedmen as if they were still slaves, in part by prohibiting them from possessing firearms and sending militiamen to search freedmen cabins for arms.

In an effort to protect the Second Amendment rights of Southern blacks, Congress passed the Freedmen's Bureau Act in 1866, which declared protection for the "full and equal benefit of all laws and proceedings concerning personal liberty, personal security, and... estate...including the constitutional right to bear arms...." It also enacted the Civil Rights Act and proposed the Fourteenth Amendment to the states for ratification as an amendment to the Constitution.

The Fourteenth Amendment declares that all persons born or naturalized in the U.S. are citizens. It also prohibits the states from abridging "the privileges and immunities of citizens," and declares that no state shall "deprive any person of life, liberty or property without due process of law," or deny to any person "the equal protection of the laws." The Freedmen's Bureau Act is key to understanding how Congress interpreted the Second Amendment some 75 years after it became part of the Constitution in 1791. It also demonstrates that the right to keep and bear arms was a fundamental right that the general clauses of the Fourteenth Amendment were intended to protect from violation by the states. Indeed, the same two-thirds of Congress that proposed the Fourteenth Amendment to the U.S. Constitution in 1866 also enacted the Freedmen's Bureau Act.

This legislative history begins on January 5, 1866,

when Senator Lyman Trumbull of Illinois introduced S. 60, the Freedmen's Bureau Bill, and S. 61, the Civil Rights Bill. To exemplify the need for legislation, black citizens of South Carolina had assembled in a convention and adopted a petition to be submitted to Congress. It stated in part:

> *We ask that, inasmuch as the Constitution of the United States explicitly declares that the right to keep and bear arms shall not be infringed—and the Constitution is the Supreme law of the land—that the late efforts of the Legislature of this State to pass an act to deprive us of arms be forbidden, as a plain violation of the Constitution. . . .*

The petition became the centerpiece of a speech on the Senate floor by Senator Charles Sumner of Massachusetts, urging protection of the freedmen, saying:

> *They also ask that government in that State shall be founded on the consent of the governed, and insist that can be done only where equal suffrage is allowed. . . . They ask also that they should have the constitutional protection in keeping arms, in holding public assemblies, and in complete liberty of speech and of the press.*

The Freedmen's Bureau Bill, including an amendment characterizing "the constitutional right to bear arms" as a "civil right," passed the House by a landslide vote of 136 to 33. Senator Trumbull, as instructed by the Committee on the Judiciary, recommended that the Senate concur in the House amendments.

Trumbull explained:

> *There is also a slight amendment in the ... section which declares that negroes and mulattoes shall have the same civil rights as white persons, and have the same security of person and estate. The House have inserted these words, "including the constitutional right of bearing arms." I think that does not alter the meaning.*

With that, Congress had passed the Freedmen's Bureau Bill. As passed, the Freedmen's Bureau Bill provided that, in areas where ordinary judicial proceedings were interrupted by the rebellion, the President should extend military protection to persons whose rights were violated. The text specified in part:

> *Wherein, in consequence of any State or local law, ordinance, police or other regulation, custom, or prejudice, any of the civil rights or immunities belonging to white persons, including the right to make and enforce contracts, to sue, be parties, and give evidence, to inherit, purchase, lease, sell, hold and convey real and personal property, and to have full and equal benefit of all laws and proceedings for the security of person and estate, including the constitutional right of bearing arms, are refused or denied to negroes, mulattoes, freedmen, refugees, or any other persons, on account of race, color, or any previous condition of slavery or involuntary*

servitude. ...

President Andrew Johnson vetoed the Freedmen's Bureau Bill, although his objections had nothing to do with the reference to "the constitutional right to bear arms." Lyman Trumbull criticized the veto, since the bill protected constitutional rights. He quoted from a letter written by Colonel Thomas in Vicksburg, Mississippi, which stated that "nearly all the dissatisfaction that now exists among the freedmen is caused by the abusive conduct of this [State] militia," which typically would "hang some freedman or search negro houses for arms."

The Senate attempted to override the veto, but mustered two votes less than the necessary two-thirds, leaving no point in the House for conducting an override vote. This was the beginning of strained relations between Congress and the President, which would snowball into an unsuccessful attempt to remove Johnson from office through impeachment.

On March 7, Representative Elliot introduced a revised version of the Freedmen's Bureau Bill. As before, it included "the constitutional right to bear arms" in the rights of personal security and personal liberty.

Debate on the Civil Rights Bill was now in full swing. Representative John A. Bingham of Ohio quoted its provisions, including its guarantee of "full and equal benefit of all laws and proceedings for the security of person and property," and explained that "the seventh and eighth sections of the Freedmen's Bureau bill enumerate the same rights and all the rights and privileges that are enumerated in the first section of this [the Civil Rights] bill. . ."

Bingham then quoted the seventh section of the first Freedmen's Bureau Bill, that provided that all persons shall "have full and equal benefit of all laws and proceedings for the security of person and estate, including the constitutional right of bearing arms. . .." The Civil Rights Bill passed both the Senate and the House, but on March 27 President Johnson vetoed it. In the override debate in the Senate, Lyman Trumbull referred to the "inherent, fundamental rights which belong to free citizens or free men in all countries, such as the rights enumerated in this bill...." He quoted a prominent legal treatise as follows:

> *The absolute rights of individuals may be resolved into the right of personal security, the right of personal liberty, and the right to acquire and enjoy property.*

The Civil Rights Bill was intended to protect these rights, which the Freedmen's Bureau Bill stated as including the right to bear arms.

The Senate successfully overrode the President's veto. The *New York Evening Post* identified "the mischiefs for which the Civil Rights bill seeks to provide a remedy" as including "attempts to prevent their [blacks] holding public assemblies. . .keeping fire-arms. . .." By April 9, the House had also overridden the President's veto, and the Civil Rights Act of 1866 became law. As enacted, § 1 provided:

> *[C]itizens, of every race and color, without regard to any previous condition of slavery or involuntary servitude. . .shall have the same right, in every State and Territory in the United States, to make and enforce*

> *contracts, to sue, be parties, and give evidence, to*
> *inherit, purchase, lease, sell, hold, and convey real*
> *and personal property, and to full and equal benefit*
> *of all laws and proceedings for the security of person*
> *and property, as is enjoyed by white citizens... That*
> *remains the law today.*

With action on the Civil Rights Act complete, Representative Eliot, on behalf of the Select Committee on Freedmen's Affairs, reported H.R. 613, the second Freedmen's Bureau Bill. As before, the new bill recognized "the constitutional right to bear arms."

Meanwhile, the proposed Fourteenth Amendment to the Constitution passed the House. On May 23, Jacob Howard of Michigan introduced it in the Senate. Senator Howard referred to "the personal rights guaranteed and secured by the first eight amendments of the Constitution; such as freedom of speech and of the press . . . the right to keep and bear arms...."

Howard explained: "The great object of the first section of this amendment is, therefore, to restrain the power of the States and compel them at all times to respect these great fundamental guarantees." No one in the Senate disputed that statement. What became the Fourteenth Amendment was clearly intended to protect the right to keep and bear arms from violation by the states.

The Freedmen's Bureau Bill was also debated in the House on May 23. Representative Eliot observed that § 8, which explicitly recognized the right to bear arms, "simply embodies the provisions of the civil rights bill, and gives to the President authority, through the Secretary of War, to extend military protection to secure those rights until the civil courts are in operation."

Eliot recited a Freedmen's Bureau report by General Clinton B. Fisk, who reported about black Union soldiers returning to their homes in Kentucky after the war ended:

> *Their arms are taken from them by the civil authorities and confiscated for the benefit of the Commonwealth. ...Thus the right of the people to keep and bear arms as provided in the Constitution is infringed.*

On May 29, the House passed H.R. 613, the Freedmen's Bureau Bill, by a vote of 96 to 32.

The House then took up the proposed Fourteenth Amendment.

While the Civil Rights Act and the Freedmen's Bureau Bill were intended to guarantee the right to keep and bear arms and other rights, the Fourteenth Amendment was needed to leave no question as to the constitutionality of such enactments or proposed enactments.

President Johnson vetoed the second Freedmen's Bureau Bill, but the House overrode the veto by 104 to 33, or 76 percent, and the Senate did so by 33 to 12, or 73 percent.

As finally passed into law on July 16, 1866, the Freedmen's Bureau Act extended the Bureau's existence for two more years. The full text of § 14 of the Act declared that the "full and equal benefit of all laws and proceedings concerning personal liberty, personal security, and . . . estate" included "the constitutional right to bear arms," and those rights "shall be secured to and enjoyed by all the citizens," who were entitled to "the free enjoyment of such immunities and rights." It is noteworthy that the same more than two-thirds of Congress that enacted this language of the Freedmen's Bureau Act also enacted similar, albeit more general, language in the Civil Rights Act, which remains on the books today.

Even more significantly, more than two-thirds of Congress adopted the Fourteenth Amendment to the Constitution and submitted it to the states for ratification. If there was any Bill of Rights guarantee that the Fourteenth Amendment was intended to protect from state infringement, it would be first and foremost the Second Amendment right to keep and bear arms.

Not even the First Amendment right to free speech was singled out for such special emphasis as was the Second Amendment. Members of the Reconstruction Congress clearly read the Second Amendment to guarantee a fundamental right of "the people," i.e., individuals.

It would be another century before the spread of the "collective right" view of the Second Amendment, under which the Amendment protects nothing more than some undefinable power of States to maintain militias or a nonsensical right to bear arms in a militia.

This first Congressional action took place in a great historical epoch just after our bloody Civil War, yet at the beginning of a civil rights revolution. The next occasion in which Congress gave homage to the Second Amendment in a statutory declaration was in one of the darkest epochs in human history for civil rights abroad. It came just before America's entry into World War II.

The Property Requisition Act of 1941: No Impairment of the Right of Any Individual to Keep and Bear Arms

That dark epoch was the Age of Totalitarianism, featuring Nazi Germany, Fascist Italy, Imperial Japan, and Communist Russia. Mass murder and genocide characterized these regimes under which depriving firearms from would-be victims was essential. The Nazi experience illustrates that point.

Americans reading the *New York Times* in November 1938 were horrified at the headlines reporting what became known as the Night of the Broken Glass: "Nazis Smash, Loot and Burn Jewish Shops and Temples Until Goebbels Calls Halt." Homes were attacked and thousands of Jewish men arrested. Essential to the success of this pogrom was the prohibition on possessing arms:

One of the first legal measures issued was an order by Heinrich Himmler, commander of all German police, forbidding Jews to possess any weapons whatever and imposing a penalty of 20 years confinement in a concentration camp upon every Jew found in possession of a weapon hereafter.

The following year, after Hitler launched World War II by attacking Poland, Americans would read about a U.S. citizen originally from Poland being executed by the Nazis for "having concealed a considerable quantity of arms and ammunition in violation of German regulations." And fast forwarding yet another year, with the collapse of France, the headlines read: "German Army Decrees Death for Those Retaining Arms and Radio Senders."

Given these events, Americans were in no mood to accept inroads on their own Second Amendment rights. Domestic prohibitionists had turned from violent crime to subversion as the excuse for watering down the right to bear arms. Not unexpectedly, they found little support. The *Times* reported:

> *In the face of pleas for compulsory registration of firearms as a defense measure against fifth columnists, the National Conference of Commissioners on Uniform State Laws voted today, by a large majority, to exclude from its proposed Uniform Pistol Act a clause compelling householders to register their weapons.... The suggested law retains the traditional right of the American citizen to keep arms as a matter of protection.*

Nonetheless, firearm registration was advocated by U.S. Attorney General Robert H. Jackson, who recommended to Congress laws making wiretapping easier, indeterminate criminal sentencing, and "a law for national registration of firearms now exempt from such listing." That would have meant that ordinary rifles, pistols, and shotguns would have been required to be registered, as were machine guns under the National Firearms Act of 1934. That proposal, made in early 1941, set off alarm bells among firearm owners and their allies in Congress.

Indeed, Jackson had argued two years earlier in the U.S. Supreme Court that the Second Amendment right is "only one which exists where the arms are borne in the militia or some other military organization provided for by law and intended for the protection of the state." In deciding *United States v. Miller* (1939), the Supreme Court disregarded that argument, ruling instead that the Second Amendment protects possession of a firearm that "is any part of the ordinary military equipment or if its use could contribute to the common defense." *Miller* focused on the nature of the arm, not on whether the possessor was a militia member.

As originally proposed in the Senate, the property requisition bill in question—S. 1579— gave the president wide powers to authorize the requisition of machinery and other property of value for the national defense on payment of just compensation. The House Committee on Military Affairs added the following qualifications to the bill:

> *That nothing herein contained shall be construed to authorize the requisition or require the registration of any firearms possessed by any individual for his personal protection or sport (and the possession of which is not prohibited nor the registration thereof required); nor shall this Act in any manner impair or infringe the right of any individual to keep and bear arms.*

The Committee Report included this explanation about the reason for adding the above provision:

> *It is not contemplated or even inferred that the President, or any executive board, agency, or officer, would trespass upon the right of the people in this respect. There appears to be no occasion for the requisition of firearms owned and maintained by the people for sport and recreation, nor is there any desire or intention on the part of the Congress or the President to impair or infringe the right of the people under section 2 [sic] of the Constitution of the United States, which reads, in part as follows: "the right of the people to keep and bear arms shall not be infringed."*

However, in view of the fact that certain totalitarian and dictatorial nations are now engaged in the willful and wholesale destruction of personal rights and liberties, our committee deem it appropriate for the Congress to expressly state that the proposed legislation shall not be construed to impair or infringe the constitutional right of the people to bear arms. In so doing, it will be manifest that, although the Congress deems it expedient to grant certain extraordinary powers to the Executive in furtherance of the common defense during critical times, there is no disposition on the part of this Government to depart from the concepts and principles of personal rights and liberties expressed in our Constitution.

While the declaration about the right to keep and bear arms was welcome, supporters of the Second Amendment were not so sure that no one contemplated future infringements. When the bill hit the House floor on August 5, Congressman Hall described what was happening abroad and anticipated violations here as follows:

Before the advent of Hitler or Stalin, who took power from the German and Russian people, measures were thrust upon the free legislatures of those countries to deprive the people of the possession and use of firearms, so that they could not resist the encroachments of such diabolical and vitriolic state police organizations as the Gestapo, the OGPU, and the Cheka. Just as sure as I am standing here today, you are going to see this measure followed by legislation, sponsored by the proponents of such encroachment upon the rights of the people, which will eventually deprive the people of their constitutional liberty which provides for the possession of firearms for the protection of their homes.

The Senate then considered the House amendment. Senator Tom Connally of Texas described it as "safe-guarding the right of individuals to possess arms." Senator Albert B. Chandler of Kentucky argued that "we have no reason to take the personal property of individuals which is kept solely for protection of their homes." Delegates to a conference committee were appointed.

The conference committee deleted the ban on registration, but kept the declaration against infringing the right to bear arms. In support of that version, Representative A.J. May, a Kentucky Democrat and conference manager, recalled remarks by the Undersecretary of War in a committee hearing:

[T]o guard against [infringement of the Second Amendment] we undertook to give these brethren here concerned about their guns the proper kind of protection, and we did it in the language of the Constitution, or as nearly as we could, and I quote from the report: "Nothing contained in this act shall be construed to impair or infringe in any manner the right of any individual to keep and bear arms.

Commenting on registration, Representative Dewey Short of Missouri explained, "The method employed by the Communists in every country that has been overthrown has been to disarm the populace, take away their firearms with which to defend themselves, in order to overthrow the

Government." Representative Paul Kilday of Texas argued the bill should forbid registration:

> *[R]emember that registration of firearms is only the first step. It will be followed by other infringements of the right to keep and bear arms until finally the right is gone.*

Noting that the Russian Communist experience taught the wisdom of Second Amendment protection for "our right to bear arms as private citizens," Representative Lyle H. Boren, an Oklahoma Democrat, averred that "the gun I own in my home is essential to maintaining the defense of my home against the aggression of lawlessness." He added about the American way of life:

> *I propose to defend it against the soldiers of a Hitler and against a government bureaucrat. All the invasions threatened against American democracy are not from without. I feel that the defense of democracy is on my doorstep and your doorstep as well as on the world's battlefields. . .. I rebel against the destruction of freedom in America under the guise of emergency.*

Rep. Kilday's motion to recommit the bill to committee then passed by 154 to 24. The resulting new conference report restored the ban on firearm registration. As passed and signed by President Franklin Roosevelt, the Property Requisition Act authorized the president to requisition broad categories of property with military uses from the private sector on payment of fair compensation, subject to the following:

Nothing contained in this Act shall be construed (1) to authorize the requisitioning or require the registration of any firearms possessed by any individual for his personal protection or sport (and the possession of which is not prohibited or the registration of which is not required by existing law), [or] (2) to impair or infringe in any manner the right of any individual to keep and bear arms....

This law bore witness that any war would be fought to preserve the Bill of Rights and other liberties, not to destroy them. And it was fitting that the Second Amendment would be declared to be of special importance as war clouds loomed, for Americans who were accustomed to keeping and bearing arms would make superior riflemen. In fact, the National Rifle Association played an instrumental role in training civilians in marksmanship throughout the war.

The Firearms Owners' Protection Act of 1986: The Right of Citizens to Keep and Bear Arms

The world had changed considerably by the time Congress enacted the Gun Control Act of 1968. A new generation of zealots pushed the envelope against constitutional rights in favor of unprecedented powers being grabbed by the federal government. The Gun Control Act intruded into traditional areas of state regulation and created numerous victimless crimes, such as making it a felony to transfer a firearm to a person in another state, to sell an unspecified number of guns without a license, or to do other harmless acts without any intent to violate the law.

By this time, prohibitionists denied that the Second Amendment protected any individual right whatsoever. U.S. Attorney General Ramsey Clark led the charge for a bill to require the registration of all firearms and to imprison those who failed to comply. After Michigan Congressman John Dingell, a Democrat, recalled how the Nazis used registration records to confiscate firearms, the Johnson administration produced a report reaching the preposterous conclusion that "there is no significant relationship between gun laws and the rise of dictators." NRA officials testifying before the committee recalled the language of the Property Requisition Act, but the prohibitionists were in denial.

The prohibitionists' registration bill was defeated. Moreover, as passed, the Gun Control Act included a preamble that eschewed any intent to burden law-abiding citizens, although it included no explicit reference to the Second Amendment. In the ensuing years, however, experience substantiated the predictions of the act's opponents that the law would be used to ensnare innocent citizens. The enforcement policies of the Bureau of Alcohol, Tobacco, and Firearms (BATF) led to numerous abuses that would be well documented in Congressional hearings beginning in the late 1970s.

Increasing awareness in Congress of the need for reform led to the enactment of the Firearms Owners' Protection Act of 1986 (FOPA). FOPA represents the third time Congress made clear by statute that the Second Amendment enshrines an individual right. Actually, FOPA declared that the existing Gun Control Act and its enforcement by BATF needed correction in light of several constitutional rights as follows:

The Congress finds that (1) the rights of citizens (A) to keep and bear arms under the second amendment to the United States Constitution; (B) to security against illegal and unreasonable searches and seizures under the fourth amendment; (C) against uncompensated taking of property, double jeopardy, and assurance of due process of law under the fifth amendment; and (D) against unconstitutional exercise of authority under the ninth and tenth amendments; require additional legislation to correct existing firearms statutes and enforcement policies; and (2) additional legislation is required to reaffirm the intent of the Congress, as expressed in section 101 of the Gun Control Act of 1968, that "it is not the purpose of this title to place any undue or unnecessary Federal restrictions or burdens on law-abiding citizens with respect to the acquisition, possession, or use of firearms appropriate to the purpose of hunting, trap shooting, target shooting, personal protection, or any other lawful activity, and that this title is not intended to discourage or eliminate the private ownership or use of firearms by law-abiding citizens for lawful purposes.

The finding in FOPA that the Second Amendment guarantees the rights of citizens to keep and bear arms was supported by a comprehensive report by the Senate's Subcommittee on the Constitution, which stated:

The conclusion is thus inescapable that the history, concept, and wording of the second amendment to the Constitution of the United States, as well as its interpretation by every major commentator and court in the first half-century after its ratification, indicates that what is protected is an individual right of a private citizen to own and carry firearms in a peaceful manner.

In FOPA's substantive reforms, Congress implemented its recognition that the Second Amendment guarantees individual rights by deregulating substantially the purchase, sale, and possession of firearms, and by requiring proof of a "willful" or "knowing" violation for conviction under the law.

FOPA further enforced Second Amendment rights and reflected Congress's traditional rejection of registration in the following provision:

No such rule or regulation prescribed after the date of the enactment of the Firearms Owners' Protection Act may require that records required to be maintained under this chapter or any portion of the contents of such records, be recorded at or transferred to a facility owned, managed, or controlled by the United States or any State or any political subdivision thereof, nor that any system of registration of firearms, firearms owners, or firearms transactions or dispositions be established.

Another important FOPA reform was the provision preempting state laws that prohibit travelers from transporting firearms throughout the United States. This reflected Congress's recognition that the Second Amendment protects the individual right to keep and bear

arms. Idaho Senator Steve Symms introduced this provision
with the explanation, "The intent of this amendment ... is
to protect the Second Amendment rights of law abiding
citizens wishing to transport firearms through States
which otherwise prohibit the possession of such weapons."
In the House, Rep. Tommy Robinson of Arkansas stated
that "our citizens have a constitutional right to bear arms
... and to travel interstate with those weapons."

FOPA, which was signed into law by President Ronald
Reagan, represents a high water mark for protection
of Second Amendment rights by the U.S. Congress.
When the Clinton administration pursued anti-Second
Amendment policies, the American electorate cleaned
house beginning in 1994, making further passage of
prohibitionist legislation in Congress difficult. At the state
level, the passage of "Right-to-Carry" laws ushered in
further defeats for the prohibitionists, who then turned to
the courts. They launched frivolous lawsuits against the
firearms industry, hoping to bankrupt it and destroy the
Second Amendment through judicial fiat.

The Protection of Lawful Commerce in Arms Act of 2005: To Preserve a Citizen's Access to Firearms

The prohibitionist attempt to bypass the legislative
process and ban guns through litigation led Congress
to enact the Protection of Lawful Commerce in Arms
Act ("PLCAA") in 2005. This Act represents the fourth
occasion in the history of the U.S. Congress in which
that body interpreted the Second Amendment to protect
individual rights. PLCAA is "An Act to prohibit civil
liability actions from being brought or continued against

manufacturers, distributors, dealers, or importers of firearms or ammunition for damages, injunctive or other relief resulting from the misuse of their products by others."

The bill was in response to more than 30 lawsuits brought by municipalities against the firearms industry aimed at ruining the industry and shutting down firearms commerce. The legislation was supported by the National Rifle Association, the Department of Defense, the National Association of Manufacturers, the U.S. Chamber of Commerce, United Mine Workers of America, and other business and union organizations. PLCAA begins with findings that go directly to the heart of the matter:

Congress finds the following:

(1) The Second Amendment to the United States Constitution provides that the right of the people to keep and bear arms shall not be infringed.

(2) The Second Amendment to the United States Constitution protects the rights of individuals, including those who are not members of a militia or engaged in military service or training, to keep and bear arms.

The Act recognizes that having arms is a constitutional right, and thus it makes no sense to sanction lawsuits against federally licensed manufacturers merely for making this constitutionally-protected product. Moreover, Congress asserted its constitutional power to protect Second Amendment rights.

Lawsuits were filed against the firearms industry for

damages and other relief for the harm caused by criminals and other third parties who misuse firearms. However, the manufacture, importation, possession, sale, and use of firearms and ammunition are heavily regulated by federal, state, and local laws.

The Supreme Court of Illinois recognized this plain fact in 2004, ruling in *Chicago v. Beretta* (2004):

> *It seems that plaintiffs seek injunctive relief from this court because relief has not been forthcoming from the General Assembly. We are reluctant to interfere in the lawmaking process in the manner suggested by plaintiffs, especially when the product at issue is already so heavily regulated by both the state and federal governments. We, therefore, conclude that there are strong public policy reasons to defer to the legislature in the matter of regulating the manufacture, distribution, and sale of firearms.*

Indeed, the federal Gun Control Act was originally passed under the Commerce Clause, adding further justification for this act. As the findings stated, businesses "are engaged in interstate and foreign commerce through the lawful design, manufacture, marketing, distribution, importation, or sale to the public of firearms or ammunition that has been shipped or transported in interstate or foreign commerce," and they should not be liable for the harm caused by unlawful misuse of firearms that function as designed and intended.

Such imposition of liability on an industry abuses the legal system, erodes public confidence in the law, "threatens the diminution of a basic constitutional right and civil liberty," destabilizes other industries in the free enterprise system of the United States, and "constitutes an unreasonable burden on interstate and foreign commerce of the United States."

Such liability actions, commenced by the federal government, various state politicians, urban officials, and gun-ban groups, were unprecedented and not a bona fide expansion of the common law. The sustaining of these actions by a "maverick" judge or jury would expand liability in a manner never contemplated by the Constitution's framers or by the federal or state legislatures. Congress's enforcement power under the Fourteenth Amendment was made clear in the further finding: "Such an expansion of liability would constitute a deprivation of the rights, privileges, and immunities guaranteed to a citizen of the United States under the Fourteenth Amendment to the United States Constitution." Those rights include the right to keep and bear arms and the right to due process of law.

The liability actions at issue "attempt to use the judicial branch to circumvent the Legislative branch of government to regulate interstate and foreign commerce through judgments and judicial decrees," undermining the separation of powers, federalism, state sovereignty and comity between the sister states.

PLCAA also included "purposes" clauses that further defined its constitutional bases. The immediate purpose was to prohibit causes of action against the firearms industry for harm caused by criminals and others who unlawfully misuse firearms.

The values of the Second Amendment were reflected in the goal "to preserve a citizen's access to a supply of firearms and ammunition for all lawful purposes, including hunting, self-defense, collecting, and competitive or recreational shooting," and "to guarantee a citizen's rights, privileges, and immunities, as applied to the States, under the Fourteenth Amendment to the United States Constitution, pursuant to section 5 of that Amendment." Section 5 is the Enforcement Clause, which allows Congress to enforce rights against state violation.

Besides preventing such lawsuits from imposing "unreasonable burdens on interstate and foreign commerce," the law also protects the First Amendment rights of members of the firearms industry, including their trade associations, "to speak freely, to assemble peaceably, and to petition the Government for a redress of their grievances."

PLCAA's substantive provision stated: "A qualified civil liability action may not be brought in any Federal or State court." Any such pending action "shall be dismissed immediately." The rest of the law defined the nature of the prohibited civil action in contrast with the types of traditional actions, which would remain unaffected. Debate on the bill focused on the substantive liability issues and proposed amendments. The propositions contained in the findings and purposes that the Second and Fourteenth Amendments guarantee an individual right to keep and bear arms went virtually uncontested.

Senator John Thune of South Dakota set the tone when he stated, "This bill is about law abiding gun owners, it is about law abiding gun dealers, it is about law abiding gun manufacturers who are having that Second Amendment right infringed upon by those who are trying to destroy an industry...." And Senator Larry Craig of Idaho—the bill's chief sponsor— maintained, "The Constitution also, I believe, imposes upon Congress the duty to protect the liberties enshrined in the Bill of Rights which includes the Second Amendment. If the firearms manufacturers are driven out of business, that Second Amendment will be nothing more than an illusion."

Opponents of firearm ownership previously denied that the Second Amendment protected any individual rights, but in this debate hypocritically attempted to wrap themselves in the Amendment. New York Senator Chuck Schumer, a consistent firearm prohibitionist, said, "The right to guns is a good thing. I support the Second Amendment." He then contradicted those words by vehemently urging defeat of the bill.

The bill would pass the Senate with 65 yeas and 31 nays, a very comfortable margin.

In House debate, Representative Lamar Smith of Texas averred that "to allow frivolous lawsuits to constrain the right of Americans to lawfully use guns is both irresponsible and unconstitutional." Noting the need to stop "this abuse of the legal process," Representative Sam Graves of Missouri explained: "This bill will protect the firearms industry from lawsuits based on the criminal or unlawful third party misuse of their products. This law is necessary to prevent a few state courts from undermining our Second Amendment rights guaranteed by the Constitution."

Representative Joe Schwarz of Michigan said it in a nutshell when he explained, "The Second Amendment was not written as a mere exercise in constitutional thought. It had a practical purpose: first, to ensure that citizens would have the tools to protect their families and their homes and, second, to ensure that an armed militia could be called up to defend the country in emergencies."

The PLCAA—with Cliff Stearns of Florida and Rick

Boucher of Virginia its chief sponsors—passed the House overwhelmingly with 283 yeas and 144 nays and was promptly signed into law by President George W. Bush. The anti-Second Amendment litigators who earlier filed the frivolous lawsuits the act was designed to eliminate, filed motions claiming that the PLCAA was unconstitutional.

The Disaster Recovery Personal Protection Act of 2006

In the wake of 2005's Hurricane Katrina, Congress acted again to affirm the right to keep and bear arms. Congress was outraged by the actions of New Orleans officials who proclaimed they would confiscate all firearms in the city—and carried out that threat.

Congress moved to protect Second Amendment rights the following year. First, the Senate adopted an amendment to the homeland security appropriations bill by Sen. David Vitter (R-La.) that barred federal agencies, or state agencies using federal funds, from confiscating firearms from law-abiding citizens during an emergency or major disaster.

This amendment was based on Sen. Vitter's bill, S. 2599, the "Disaster Recovery Personal Protection Act," which included a congressional finding that "Congress has repeatedly recognized [the Second Amendment] as protecting an individual right." That bill was broader—not only barring confiscations, but also allowing citizens to file civil rights suits in federal court, for any type of relief the court can grant, including an order to return the firearm.

The Vitter Amendment passed by an overwhelming margin of 84-16. Its opponents were a "Who's Who" of anti-gun extremists, including Sens. Hillary Clinton, Frank Lautenberg, Dianne Feinstein, Chuck Schumer and Dick Durbin. And under the unblinking eye of the C-SPAN cameras, Sen. John Kerry voted against the Vitter amendment. Minutes later he reversed course and voted for it.

The House followed up by taking action on H.R. 5013, sponsored by Rep. Bobby Jindal (R-La.). Rep. Jindal's bill was the same as Sen. Vitter's original bill, and included the same finding about the Second Amendment.

As in previous debates, the members of the House spoke eloquently about the meaning of the Second Amendment. Rep. Randy Kuhl of New York, a cosponsor of the amendment, noted its purpose of ensuring "that law-abiding citizens can continue to protect themselves, their loved ones, their businesses, and their property as guaranteed by the Second Amendment during disasters." Rep. Don Young of Alaska noted the bill "precludes the government from taking away what is my cherished personal right to protect those I love." And responding to critics of the bill, Rep. Young added, "Some would say it is not necessary, it will not happen again. I have been around here long enough to … never say it will not happen again." Anti-gun leaders in the House mustered fewer than a hundred votes against the Jindal bill, which passed 322-99.

A conference committee on the final homeland security bill adopted the broad, permanent House language, and President George W. Bush signed it into law. Though the final product did not include the findings about the Second Amendment, the message was clear: where necessary, Congress would step in to enforce the right of the people to keep and bear arms.

Future history will determine if Congress will deem it necessary once again to protect the Second Amendment rights of American citizens.

As the branch elected by the people, the U.S. Congress fulfills its proper function when it declares and protects the constitutional rights of the people. This role is essential to the checks and balances necessary to prevent power from being concentrated in one branch of government. Great weight should be accorded to the repeated determinations by Congress, over a long historical period and in vastly different historical circumstances, that the right to keep and bear arms is a fundamental, individual right that government may not infringe.

CHAPTER 4:
Owning and Carrying Firearms For Self-Defense

Cicero, the great Roman statesman, lawyer and political theorist said nearly 2,000 years ago: "If our lives are endangered by plots or violence or armed robbers or enemies, any and every method of protecting ourselves is morally right."

Jurist Sir William Blackstone, whose *Commentaries on the Laws of England* is frequently quoted by U.S. courts as the definitive pre-Revolutionary War source of common law, observed that the English Bill of Rights recognized "the right of having and using arms for self-preservation and defense" as intended "to protect and maintain inviolate the three great and primary rights," the first of which is "personal security."

Approaching the right to self-defense from another angle, Jeffrey R. Snyder reminds us in his seminal essay, "A Nation of Cowards," of a sermon given in Philadelphia in 1747 that unequivocally equated the failure to defend oneself with suicide:

> *He that suffers his life to be taken from him by one that hath no authority for that purpose, when he might preserve it by defense, incurs the Guilt of self murder since God hath enjoined him to seek the continuance of his life, and Nature itself teaches every creature to defend itself.*

So it should come as no surprise that the U.S. constitution, 44 state constitutions, common law, and the laws of all 50 states recognize the right to use arms in self-defense. Additionally, Congress stated in both the Gun Control Act (1968) and Firearms Owners' Protection Act (1986) that it did not intend to "place any undue or unnecessary Federal restrictions or burdens on law-abiding citizens with respect to the acquisition, possession, or use of firearms appropriate to … personal protection, or any other lawful activity."

Right-to-Carry (RTC) laws respect the right to self-defense by allowing citizens to carry firearms for protection. There are 40 RTC states: 36 have "shall issue" laws, which require that carry permits be issued to applicants who meet uniform standards established by the state legislature. Alabama, Connecticut and Iowa have fairly-administered "discretionary-issue" carry permit systems. Vermont respects the right to carry without a permit. (Alaska, which has a shall-issue provision for purposes of permit reciprocity with other states, adopted a no-permit-required law in 2003.) Of the 10 non-RTC states, eight have restrictively-administered discretionary-issue systems, while Wisconsin and Illinois prohibit carrying altogether.

Evidence supporting the value of Right-to-Carry laws and the high standard of conduct among persons who carry firearms lawfully is overwhelming and continues to mount. In his book, *More Guns, Less Crime*, Prof. John R. Lott, Jr. provides the most comprehensive study of firearm laws ever conducted. With an economist's eye, Lott examined a large volume of data ranging from gun ownership polls to FBI crime rate data for each of the nation's 3,045 counties over an 18-year period. He included in his analysis many variables that might explain the level of crime—factors such as income, poverty, unemployment, population density, arrest rates, conviction rates and length of prison sentences.

With 54,000 observations and hundreds of variables available over the 1977 to 1994 period, Lott's research amounts to the largest data set that has ever been compiled for any study of crime, let alone for the study of gun control. And, unlike many gun control advocates who masquerade as researchers, Lott willingly made his complete data set available to any academic who requested it.

"Many factors influence crime," Lott writes, "with arrest and conviction rates being the most important. However, non discretionary concealed-handgun laws are also important, and they are the most cost-effective means of reducing crime."

Non discretionary, or "shall-issue" carry permit laws reduce violent crime for two reasons. They reduce the number of attempted crimes, because criminals can't tell which potential victims are armed and can defend themselves. Secondly, national crime victimization surveys show that victims who use firearms to defend themselves are statistically less likely to be injured. In short, carry laws deter crime, because they increase the criminal's risk of doing business.

Lott found "a strong negative relationship between the number of law-abiding citizens with permits and the crime rate—as more people obtain permits there is a greater decline in violent crime rates." Further, he found that the value of carry laws increases over time. "For each additional year that a concealed handgun law is in effect the murder rate declines by 3%, rape by 2% and robberies by over 2%," Lott writes.

The benefits of concealed handguns are not limited to those who carry them. Others "get a 'free ride' from the crime fighting efforts of their fellow citizens," Lott finds. And the benefits are "not limited to people who share the characteristics of those who carry the guns."

Lott devotes an entire chapter of his book to rebutting attacks leveled at his research and at him personally. Such attacks, unfortunately, are common. Prof. Gary Kleck, a criminologist at Florida State University, explains why:

> *Battered by a decade of research contradicting the central factual premises underlying gun control, advocates have apparently decided to fight more exclusively on an emotional battlefield, where one terrorizes one's targets into submission rather than honestly persuading them with credible evidence.*

Kleck's own award-winning research has found that "robbery and assault victims who used a gun to resist were less likely to be attacked or to suffer an injury than those who used any other methods of self-protection or those who did not resist at all."

In the 1990s, Kleck and colleague Marc Gertz found that guns were used for self-protection each year in the U.S. as frequently as 2.5 million times annually. The late Marvin E. Wolfgang, self-described as "as strong a gun-control advocate as can be found among the criminologists in this country," who wanted to "eliminate all guns from the civilian population and maybe even from the police," said, "The methodological soundness of the current Kleck and Gertz study is clear. I cannot further debate it. . . . I cannot fault their methodology."

Further, a study for the Dept. of Justice found that 34% of felons had been "scared off, shot at, wounded or captured by an armed victim," and 40% of felons have not committed crimes, fearing potential victims were armed.

Speaking directly to Right-to-Carry, law professor and firearms issue researcher David Kopel notes:

> *Whenever a state legislature first considers a concealed-carry bill, opponents typically warn of horrible consequences. Permit-holders will slaughter each other in traffic disputes, while would-be Rambos shoot bystanders in incompetent attempts to thwart crime. But within a year of passage, the issue usually drops off the news media's radar screen, while gun-control advocates in the legislature conclude that the law wasn't so bad after all.*

The Texas experience is a case in point. Before Gov. George W. Bush was able to sign Texas' carry law, predictions of a return to the Wild West were also made. But honest public servants who initially opposed the law have stepped forth to admit they were wrong. John B. Holmes, Harris County's district attorney, said that he thought the legislation presented "a clear and present danger to law-abiding citizens by placing more handguns on our streets. Boy was I wrong. Our experience in Harris County, and indeed statewide, has proven my initial fears absolutely groundless."

And this from Glen White, president of the Dallas Police Association: "All the horror stories I thought would come to pass didn't happen....I think it's worked out well, and that says good things about the citizens who have permits. I'm a convert."

More and more Americans have come to understand that in the real world there is no such thing as a "crime-free zone," and that violent crime can occur anywhere at anytime. They also recognize that they can be severely injured or even killed in seconds. They have taken the responsibility for protecting their lives into their own hands.

That was a choice that was stolen away from many American citizens in August 2005. When Hurricane Katrina caused devastation along much of the north-central Gulf Coast of the U.S., the most severe loss of life and property damage occured in New Orleans, which flooded after catastrophic failure of the levee system.

New Orleans became the first venue in America to disarm its peaceable citizens house by house—at gunpoint. Nothing brought home the sheer terror of it all more than two broadcast video segments: one on ABC News and another on Fox News Channel.

Opening with scenes of police and National Guardsmen entering homes on a block-by-block search, you cannot watch the ABC piece without fear and anger. Everybody who has seen it had the same reaction—the Constitution had been trashed. This was supposed to be a humanitarian effort, not a shoot-to-kill military operation.

Anyone who might think shoot-to-kill is overblown should imagine having a locked and loaded M16 rifle or M4 carbine leveled at him by a youthful guardsman with fear in his eyes. Then imagine someone shouting, "He has a gun!"

This is the worst case for honest gun owners come true, giving lie to false promises that forced gun confiscation would never happen in America.

With images of police and guardsmen clearing rooms, shouldered M16s at the ready, the ABC reporter explained that they enter homes "with guns drawn with instructions to disarm anyone inside." Then the New Orleans police chief says, "No one will be able to be armed. We're going to take all weapons." Remember, this has always been the endgame of New Orleans politicians, who were first in line to take a crack at suing the firearms industry out of existence.

In the ABC broadcast, young men are sitting on a curb with arms handcuffed behind their backs, surrounded by heavily armed police. Their "crime," as explained by the ABC reporter: "[H]omeowners had armed themselves to protect their mansions. Residents were handcuffed on the ground, and in the end, police took their weapons but let them stay in their homes."

In the close of the ABC footage, a very young guardsman says, "Walking up and down these streets you don't want to have to think about the stuff you are going to have to do. If somebody pops around the corner ...." Off camera, the reporter interrupts and says, "You mean shoot an American."

The Americans this young man might have shot were not looters; they were not criminals. They are brave people who simply refused to obey an order by the same local authorities who indefensibly failed to protect them.

Keep in mind, those officials—who ordered every decent citizen of their city to be forcibly disarmed—also sent tens of thousands of residents whose homes were destroyed to endure the living hell of the Superdome and the Convention Center; where people died or were murdered; where bodies rotted; where medical practitioners were frightened away; where gang members killed, robbed and raped at will. All of this with virtually no police presence for a week.

For citizens in neighborhoods spared the flooding and wind damage from the hurricane, the evacuation order made no sense. And arming themselves to protect their persons, families, homes and communities from roving criminal predators made perfect sense. Self-protection is the most basic human right of all.

To see the National Guard troops in this ABC segment was to see them on a war footing. They were edgy. Fearful. But this wasn't war. This was a natural disaster involving innocent Americans who were victims of nature. These are Americans who chose to be armed so that they would not further become victims of criminal violence.

Many of these people who stayed in their relatively unscathed neighborhoods couldn't bring themselves to abandon their pets, their possessions. They feared leaving more than staying. Think of being disarmed at gunpoint by the very people who you thought had come to help.

For any level of government—state, local or federal— to disarm these good people in their own homes using the threat of imminent deadly force is unthinkable.

The Fox broadcast brought that message home with incredible force. Seeing a burly police officer body slam a frail, elderly woman who was showing officers her home protection gun—a little Colt Police Positive—is almost beyond imagination. Her gun was taken, and she was hauled out of her home.

Law enforcement? No. Tyranny. Clear and simple. And it is a tyranny that must be stopped—and never allowed to happen again.

NRA is committed to ensuring that innocent Americans always have the means to defend themselves in their homes and neighborhoods. NRA has fought to enact laws to prohibit state and federal authorities from seizing firearms from innocent citizens under a state of emergency due to a natural disaster or terrorist attack.

Within a year of Hurricane Katrina hitting the Gulf Coast, Congress passed the NRA-backed Disaster Recovery Personal Protection Act. This bill amended federal emergency laws to prohibit federal, state, and local authorities from confiscating lawfully-owned firearms during emergencies or disasters. (See Chapter 3 for more details on this historic legislation).

While many remember 2005 as the year of Katrina, another strong storm began blowing across America at that time, and its winds still show no signs of abating. In the teeth of this storm stood a criminal justice system that for far too long seemed to favor the rights of criminals over the rights of crime victims.

In April 2005, the Florida legislature acted to fortify the right to self-defense, passing overwhelmingly (unanimously in the Senate and 94-20 in the House) a "Castle Doctrine" law. The new law removes the "duty to retreat" when citizens are outside of their homes and where they have a legal right to be. It says that if a criminal breaks into your home or occupied vehicle or a place where you are camping overnight, for example, you may presume that he is there to do bodily harm and use any force, including deadly force, to protect yourself from a violent attack. Floridians who defend themselves from criminal attack are shielded by the new law from criminal prosecution and from civil suits brought by their attackers.

In testifying for the bill, Marion P. Hammer, executive director of Unified Sportsmen of Florida, said: "No one knows what is in the twisted mind of a violent criminal. You can't expect a victim to wait before taking action to protect herself and say: 'Excuse me, Mr. Criminal, did you drag me into this alley to rape and kill me or do you just want to beat me up and steal my purse?'"

In two years following Florida's lead, an additional 18 states passed "Castle Doctrine" laws, recognizing that self-defense is and must remain the bedrock principle of the Second Amendment.

Chapter 5:
The United Nations: Choking Off The Second Amendment in the United States

Did the work of the National Rifle Association members in the 2000 election matter? If Al Gore had won that election—and he would have won if the NRA had not put George W. Bush over the top in West Virginia, Missouri, Florida, Arkansas, and Tennessee—then the 2001 U.N. anti-gun conference would have had an entirely different result.

Rather than drawing a line in the sand against a binding international treaty, the U.S. delegation would have enthusiastically supported an extremely repressive treaty.

The Clinton-Gore administration was well aware—as a Kerry administration would also have been—of how effectively the U.N. can be used to impose extreme gun laws in the U.S. During the Clinton-Gore administration, when the draft protocol for the 2001 convention was being prepared, it was the Colombian and Mexican delegations, not the American delegation, that offered optional language recognizing that some countries have legitimate traditions of sporting and other gun use.

Now you may wonder, what harm could signing a bad treaty do? After all, the U.S. Constitution requires that treaties be ratified by a two-thirds vote of the U.S. Senate. There are many ways in which extreme U.N. gun laws could be enforced in the U.S., even without ratification of a repressive treaty by the U.S. Senate.

First of all, the president could call the document an "Agreement" rather than a "Treaty." Then, instead of needing two-thirds of the Senate, the document would simply need a majority in the U.S. House and Senate for approval. This tactic is precisely how President Bill Clinton convinced Congress to ratify the North American Free Trade Agreement (NAFTA), which never could have won two-thirds' support in the Senate.

As a practical matter, if a president's party controls both houses of Congress, it is nearly impossible to stop him from building a majority for anything he wants—if the president is willing to commit every resource he has to getting the bill passed. That is how the Clinton gun ban was approved in 1994—by a Democratic president applying extreme pressure (both threats and promises) to normally pro-gun Democratic legislators.

Another back-door approach to extreme gun control would be an international treaty that, on its face, looks innocuous. The treaty might simply contain language about preventing arms transfers to criminals, and perhaps some requirements that countries enact strict controls on commercial firearms exports. (U.S. export controls are already the strictest in the world.) Then, a president might convince a majority of both houses—or two-thirds of the Senate—to make the document into law, since it appears to be harmless to U.S. rights.

The U.N. has a very long history of convincing nations to sign on to treaties with moderate, sensible language, and then—after ratification—twisting that language to impose extremist results.

Consider, as just one example, the U.N. Convention on the Rights of the Child. It is being reinterpreted by U.N. bureaucrats in ways never agreed to by the governments that signed the convention. According to the U.N.'s Committee on the Rights of the Child, the convention means that all children, no matter how young, have—with no need for parental consent, or even in opposition to parental wishes—an unlimited right to reproductive and sexual services, and to freedom of association.

Obviously none of the 191 ratifying nations meant to accept such a radical destruction of parental rights. But, as one U.N. watchdog notes: "In light of such Committee actions, U.N. delegates fear it is impossible for countries to know what they are endorsing when they ratify international treaties. What is more, essential power may no longer rest with those who write treaties, but with those who get to interpret them."

Thus, any U.N. firearms treaty that becomes law in the U.S. could become a platform for the imposition of extremist gun control, with U.N. bureaucrats, not U.S. voters, making the decisions.

Even worse, U.N. gun prohibition can be imposed in the U.S. without any form of approval from Congress. Let's suppose a gun-ban president, say Hillary Clinton, signs a U.N. anti-gun treaty, for ratification by Congress.

Now consider the Vienna Convention on Treaties, which has been ratified by the U.S. It provides the rules for how nations are supposed to abide by international treaties. One of the rules of the Vienna Convention is that once a nation has signed (not ratified, just signed) a treaty, the nation may not undermine the treaty.

So, relying on the signed but unratified treaty,

President Hillary Clinton could start issuing executive orders to impose various gun laws because, she could claim, without executive orders the U.S. would be illegally undermining the treaty.

Would American courts enforce the Second Amendment to defend our rights against international gun control—either in the form of a treaty, or in the form of executive orders based on an unratified treaty?

Not necessarily. It's true that a treaty, even if ratified by the U.S. Senate, cannot directly repeal constitutional rights. Many judges, however, would interpret the Second Amendment so narrowly that the right to arms would always give way to the requirements of any "gun-control" treaty. Such judges believe in what they call a "living Constitution"—but what they really mean is a "dead Constitution." They reject a Constitution whose text and intent are the law of the land, favoring instead a Constitution that has no enduring meaning, but can be changed on the whim of a judge, based on the judge's determination of social policy.

Even worse, the very existence of international gun-control treaties, even treaties that are never signed or ratified by the U.S., provides judges with a pretext for choking off Second Amendment rights.

The fact that many nations have nearly obliterated gun owners' rights and the right to self-defense is already an important reason, according to some judges, for interpreting the Second Amendment into protecting nothing at all. The existence of international gun control treaties reinforces their argument that the Second Amendment can be shriveled out of existence.

Supreme Court Justice Stephen Breyer told ABC's

George Stephanopoulos that we must rise to "the challenge" of making sure the U.S. Constitution "fits into the governing documents of other nations." In the case of *Knight v. Florida*, Justice Breyer wrote that it was "useful" to consider the death penalty jurisprudence in India, Jamaica, and Zimbabwe.

The notion that the U.S. Supreme Court should be guided by courts from the thuggish dictatorship of Robert Mugabe in Zimbabwe is outrageous.

And while Jamaica and India have every right to enact their own laws for their own nations, so does the U.S. The American people will no longer be sovereign if courts start interpreting the U.S. Constitution based on the laws of other nations.

In *Grutter v. Bollinger*, in which the Supreme Court was asked to interpret the Fourteenth Amendment to the U.S. Constitution and the federal Civil Rights Act of 1964, Justices Ruth Bader Ginsburg, David Souter, and Breyer cited the Convention on the Elimination of Discrimination Against Women—an international treaty that has never been ratified by the U.S. And Justice Ginsburg, in a speech to the American Constitution Society (a group of left-wing legal activists and academics), celebrated the Supreme Court abandoning the "Lone Ranger mentality" and being "more open to comparative and international law perspectives."

In the death penalty case *Atkins v. Virginia*, Justice John Paul Stevens wrote the opinion for the majority of the Court, and cited an amicus brief from the European Union. He quoted the E.U.'s statement that "within the world community, the imposition of the death penalty for crimes committed by mentally retarded offenders is overwhelmingly disapproved."

So according to Justice Stevens—and a majority of the Court—the European Union's disapproval is a good enough reason for the Supreme Court to change the meaning of our Constitution. The danger to the Second Amendment is quite obvious, since the E.U. also strongly disapproves of the American right to arms and the American right to self defense.

Even more perilous, the international gun prohibition movement needs neither a treaty nor the cooperation of even one branch of our government in order to destroy the Second Amendment.

Formal legal documents—such as treaties, conventions, agreements, and declarations—are one source of international law. But international law is also based on "norms" or "customary law." In recent decades, activist lawyers have become extremely adept at fabricating norms and customary law out of thin air. Courts do not always go along with these nonsense-on-stilts arguments, but some could.

So even without a treaty, gun prohibitionists can argue in U.S. courts that international norms compel the court to interpret the Second Amendment, and the states' individual constitutional rights to arms, restrictively.

More ominously, a supposed international norm against civilian gun ownership—especially gun ownership for defense against criminals or a tyrannical government—could also be raised in a foreign court. In *The Second Amendment and Global Gun Control*, attorney Joseph Bruce Alonso describes how U.S. gun manufacturers could be sued in foreign courts.

In a foreign court, the Second Amendment would

provide no defense. Nor would any of the due process protections of the U.S. Constitution be applicable. American statutes such as the Protection of Lawful Commerce in Firearms Act would be irrelevant.

The prospect of destroying our Second Amendment through foreign lawsuits is already being developed. In the fall of 2005, the national government of Canada urged Canada's provincial governments to sue American gun companies in Canadian courts. (So far, none of the provinces have acted, but they could change their minds at any time, based on political calculation.)

Importantly, if one day U.S. gun controls are deemed a human rights violation, you can bet a wide variety of legal theories will spring up under which the American firearms industry could be sued in foreign or international courts.

University of Minnesota law professor Barbara Frey has been appointed the U.N. Special Rapporteur on the relationship between guns and human rights. In her role, she has served as an active ally of the gun prohibition movement. For example, in early 2005, she participated in a strategy session in Brazil in which various non-government organizations plotted how to pass a total gun prohibition referendum in that nation in October. The conference was sponsored by Brazil and Via Rio, the group that pushed the handgun ban.

At the Brazil conference, Frey argued—and remember, she was speaking in her official capacity as the U.N.'s Special Rapporteur supplying an official report to the U.N. Human Rights Commission—that it is a human rights violation for a government not to impose some of the gun-control laws she favors. These controls include, but are not limited to, licensing for all gun owners, "safe storage" (that is, "lock-up-your-gun safety laws" preventing guns from being used in an emergency against an intruder), "and other appropriate measures to remove unwanted small arms from circulation."

Frey, IANSA, and the rest of the U.N. gun-ban bureaucracy are also working on creating a claim that international law already forbids supplying arms to a serious abuser of human rights. The theory could, perhaps, lead to the supplier being sued in a foreign court, or even criminally prosecuted in the International Criminal Court.

Of course, it would be a good idea if the theory would be deployed against governments that actually are gross abusers of human rights—such as Sudan, Zimbabwe, or North Korea. But remember, according to the U.N., the worst human rights abuser in the world is Israel, and the fourth worst is the U.S.

Frey also says "there is a need to explore the boundaries of the right to self-defense as a general principle of criminal law and its specific application to small arms possession and use." Since Frey is a member of IANSA—whose president, Rebecca Peters, denies that people have any right to self-defense, or to own firearms for self-defense—it is not hard to predict the result of the reexamination that Frey and the U.N. are conducting.

In the Orwellian world of the U.N., America's first freedom amounts to a human rights violation. The total gun prohibition that the U.N. has imposed on other nations, leaving them helpless against criminals, is precisely what the U.N. wants to impose on the U.S. After all, as Peters puts it, the United States has no right to be different from other countries.

The U.N. is the most lethal threat ever to our Second Amendment rights. Although we avoided the worst possible results at the summer 2006 U.N. anti-gun conference in New York City, the U.N. and the international gun prohibition movement will continue their war against the Second Amendment. The danger to human rights in the U.S. and around the world grows more deadly every year. Already many thousands of people around the globe have been victims of genocide, because of the "success" of the U.N.'s war on gun ownership.

To close our eyes and pretend "it can't happen here" would literally be a fatal error. The next chapter describes just how close we came to seeing it happen in America.

Chapter 6:
The U.N. Gun Ban Treaty

It was 1996, in the dark days of the Clinton administration, when I first began to sound the alarm to the unsuspecting gun owners of our nation.

The gun-ban lobby, having been forced to a standstill in Congress, was looking for new avenues on which to attack our Second Amendment rights. At the same time, the vast apparatus of the United Nations and its associated non-governmental organizations was fresh off a global campaign to ban land mines and looking for a new rallying cry. It was 1997 when a U.N. panel of "government experts on small arms" delivered a formal recommendation for a global conference to be held in the near future.

The goal? A global treaty to restrict "small arms and light weapons."

The U.N. had plunged headlong into the gun-ban business.

Upping the ante in 1999, the U.N. issued another demand for a small arms conference to be held in 2001. They were making a high-stakes bet on the outcome of the 2000 presidential election. They were counting on Al Gore to not only take the Oval Office, but also encourage the creation of the global gun-ban manifesto as the next natural step of the relentless Clinton-Gore drive to destroy Americans' Second Amendment rights. And so the conference was slated for July 2001, to make sure that the newly elected Gore would have enough time to install the anti-gun lobby's operatives into key positions with authority over the United States' negotiating positions.

Self-appointed social engineers all over the world were silently cheering for the Gore campaign, and the major funders of the global gun-ban movement poured their resources into shadowy political operations intended to ensure a Gore victory.

The plan was simple, and the bets were laid. But the silk-stocking set forgot to account for a single, major political force that would come to play a pivotal role in the presidential election—the National Rifle Association, and more importantly, its base of grassroots supporters.

NRA president Charlton Heston and I went on the road for weeks leading up to the presidential election. In every city we visited, our message was simple: our gun rights could not survive another four years of Clinton-Gore assaults. We took our message to the heartland and to the battleground states. Just before the elections, we held our last rallies in Tennessee and Arkansas—just to make sure that the voters who had first elected Clinton and Gore would know exactly how far their favored sons had strayed from their home state's political values. At every venue, capacity crowds jammed shoulder-to-shoulder to hear our message and to join our battle cry in unison—to "Vote Freedom First" and elect George W. Bush to the U.S. presidency.

The outcome is now well-charted in history. Against the backdrop of the agonizing weeks spent on the Florida recounts, analysts were musing over results that indicated vast departures from past voting history. Against all odds and predictions, George W. Bush had won Arkansas, Tennessee, and three other states, states that Bill Clinton himself credited the NRA with helping President Bush to win. Once the Supreme Court put an end to the partisanship in Florida, the victor was declared.

We were all exhausted for weeks. It had taken every penny we could muster to pay for the advertising, direct mail, phone banks, and political rallies. It had taken every ounce of personal energy to keep up the breakneck pace of weeks of political rallies, some of them held in three different cities per day. And it had taken every last vote we could summon from the nation's sportsmen to Vote Freedom First, defeat Al Gore, and protect our rights from another four years of withering assault in the nation's capital.

But the U.N. was another story entirely.

It was too late for the U.N. puppet-masters to beat a strategic retreat. The plan for the gun-ban conference and treaty continued right on pace. The global gun-ban forces planned to avenge their defeated champion Al Gore.

They knew that the Bush administration would not let them run roughshod over the constitutionally guaranteed freedoms of American citizens, so they were going to turn the event into a media circus.

And then they made another bet. The demands issuing from the conference would include another conference in 2006, for another bite of the apple after the 2004 presidential elections. And there we were about to witness the U.N.'s second concerted effort to strip the Second Amendment from our Constitution. This time, however, we wouldn't have to worry about the drafting of a wide-ranging treaty to demand that our rights be sacrificed on the altar of global political correctness.

Because this time, the treaty was already in place. It had been for five years.

In July 2001, the conference stage was set, and I traveled to New York City just to observe the spectacle. The official title of the meeting was "United Nations Conference on the Illicit Trade in Small Arms and Light Weapons in All its Aspects"—not the first or last time the U.N. crowd would demonstrate its passion for long, ambiguous phrases to describe the proceedings.

You see, there really are no definitions at the U.N. Specific meanings for terms of discussion would force the diplomats to abandon their rambling rhetoric. Diplomacy as practiced at the U.N. includes intentional vagueness, apparently intended to spare the diplomats from being forced to make concrete decisions over agreed-upon terms. There are no definitions, and there are no votes. The only progress made by the body as a whole would come in the celebrated process of "consensus." Consensus, to my observation, meant wearing down your opponents with media ambushes and other confrontations designed purely to reduce resistance.

But it was immediately clear to me what the terms "small arms and light weapons" meant to the U.N. delegates. As I climbed the steps to the U.N. building on that morning, I came across the single most prominent statue on the plaza. It shows a revolver with its barrel twisted into a pretzel.

And when I stepped in the doors, I saw another special piece of "artwork" commissioned specifically for the conference. It consisted of more than 7,000 rifles, pistols, and shotguns, crushed into the shape of a cube. Over the cube shined a single light from above, "epitomizing hope for change in the future." Other themed artwork designed to inspire the conference included murals entitled "Guns

'R Us" and the "Mural of Pain," the latter showing photos and drawings of "victims of gun violence."

There were no pictures of mortars, shoulder-fired rockets, heavy crew served machine guns, or anything else you and I might consider to be "small arms and light weapons." There was no criticism of rogue military forces or genocidal governments. The conference and its artwork focused only on the "scourge of small arms" and the "flood of weaponry," with all fingers pointed to the United States and our "lax gun laws" as their source.

No, the target of the conference was revolvers, pistols, shotguns, and rifles. Your guns. And your rights.

The day before the conference opened, the spectacle was fully underway.

And what a show! Remember, the staff and diplomats at the U.N. are outnumbered many fold by the representatives of non-governmental organizations, or NGOs. Thousands of these groups are accredited at the U.N., and make a full-time living from pressing their demands before the body. The largest and most influential NGOs serve as puppet-masters for delegates who support their extremist agendas. With supreme arrogance, the NGOs refer to themselves and their pet delegates at the U.N. as "civil society."

Media grandstanding is part and parcel of their program. Even before the conference was officially underway, supporters took to the streets with giant protest puppets, most depicting the newly elected President Bush in a less-than-flattering light. The U.N. itself made its plaza available for a daylong series of speeches, exhibits, displays, posters, and video-loop "documentaries."

The crowning touch was a page from the U.S. anti-gun lobby playbook, the so-called Silent March, where thousands of shoes were arranged on a red carpet. There were candles and incense, and singing, and much holding of hands. It had all the hallmarks of protest marches in the nation's capital, complete with hundreds of barefoot NGO activists, except here the protesters were also the professionals. The next day, they would move into the U.N. building in force, and play a major role in the outcome of the negotiations.

Let's talk about what happens during a U.N. conference. Most folks probably envision the typical shot of the U.N. chamber, with delegates plugged into headphones offering translation to their native tongue. This scene did play out during the conference, but it is only the smallest part of the proceedings.

The bulk of the theater takes place outside the U.N. building, with staged events and media productions built around themes assigned to different days of discussion. The first day of the gun-ban conference was called "Small Arms Destruction Day," complete with a U.N.-issued handbook "to aid those in charge of such destruction." Countries around the world were encouraged to destroy "confiscated, collected, seized, or surplus" firearms and to invite the local media for maximum exposure.

And the U.N. helpfully published a daily "Disarmament Times" newspaper to help keep activists up to speed on the day's events. A total of 119 of the approved 177 NGOs registered for the conference, dispatching 380 representatives.

Some of those NGOs were umbrella groups, such as the International Action Network on Small Arms (IANSA), which in turn includes more than 500 other NGOs. That made for plenty of street theater during the conference.

Back in the U.N. headquarters building, the discussions proceeded at several levels. The only visible evidence of the conference came in the form of regular speeches offered by delegates of participating countries. These vague, rambling speeches touched on various issues within the negotiations, occasionally offering a nation's perspective but still couched in blurred, equivocal rhetoric that seemed essentially meaningless. The U.N. also allowed the NGOs to make their own presentations to the delegates, a process that reminded me of the frequent sight on Capitol Hill of a lone congressman speaking to an empty chamber.

The real action went on in dozens of conference rooms deep in the bowels of the building. That's where hundreds of staff-level negotiators from the major participating nations hammered out specific language to propose to their country's delegates upstairs. The United States had representatives present from its headquarters U.N. staff, the Department of State, the Department of Defense, and dozens of smaller agencies. But it's impossible to know what's going on in these discussions, as they are closed to the public and to NGOs as well. In fact, the entire two final days of the conference were conducted in closed session, when the major nations finally began to negotiate in earnest over the final document.

It struck me as more than mildly ironic that the U.N., an institution purportedly striving for democracy and representative government all over the globe, would conduct its business behind an unyielding façade of official silence. Where was the outrage? My professional lifetime has been devoted to affecting the policy decisions of elected lawmakers. In the 50 state legislatures and U.S. Congress, not even our fiercest enemies ever tried to deprive us of the opportunity to witness debate and affect the outcome of votes. Here, there would be no voting. There would be no opportunity to witness the real debate over the provisions of the treaty. And there was certainly no way to lobby the delegates for or against anything in particular, if by chance you could find out what was really under debate behind closed doors.

The process needed a central focus, a starting point from which to draw our battle lines. And that's when Undersecretary of State John Bolton showed up.

Undersecretary Bolton was then fairly new to the job. Appointed by President George W. Bush, Bolton had a reputation as a hard-liner in foreign policy, one that was well-deserved. Bolton was once asked, under questioning from a congressman, to explain his approach to negotiating foreign policy with other nations. The congressman suggested to Bolton that perhaps a carrot-and-stick approach would be more fruitful than a hard-line position. Bolton cut him off, saying curtly, "I don't do carrots."

But he brought his stick to the U.N., appearing before the delegates on July 9, 2001. He began his address with the typical flourishes of the U.N. idiom, addressing the audience as "Excellencies and distinguished colleagues." But diplomacy stopped there, and Bolton went directly to the heart of the matter, first attempting to force some definitions into the process.

"Small arms and light weapons, in our understanding, are the strictly military arms—automatic rifles, machine guns, shoulder-fired missile and rocket systems, light mortars," he said. "We separate these military arms from firearms such as hunting rifles and pistols, which are commonly owned and used by citizens in many countries."

Bolton went on: "As U.S. Attorney General John Ashcroft has said, 'just as the First and Fourth Amendments secure individual rights of speech and security respectively, the Second Amendment protects an individual right to keep and bear arms.' We therefore do not begin with the presumption that all small arms and light weapons are the same, or that they are problematic."

Bolton then outlined the opposition of the United States to many of the treaty's proposed elements, saying:

> *We do not support measures that would constrain legal trade and legal manufacturing of small arms and light weapons.... We do not support the promotion of international advocacy activity by international or non-governmental organizations, particularly when those political or policy views advocated are not consistent with the views of all member states.... We do not support measures that prohibit the civilian possession of small arms [and] the United States will not join consensus on a final document that contains measures contrary to our Constitutional right to bear arms.*

He closed by calling the opposition's bet on a 2006 conference:

> *The United States also will not support a mandatory Review Conference, which serves only to institution-alize and bureaucratize this process. ...Neither will we commit to begin negotiations and reach agreement on any legally binding instruments, the feasibility and*

necessity of which may be in question and in need of review over time.

Timid applause greeted the end of his remarks, but many of the delegates were silently fuming. Bolton had just slammed the door on U.S. participation in the holy grail of the conference—a legally binding global treaty, designed and intended to restrict the rights of American citizens.

But again, the U.N. would not be so easily defeated. The forces behind the gun-ban treaty retreated overnight to recalculate their strategy. By the next morning, their tactic was clear: proceed under the framework established by Bolton's comments, continue negotiations over treaty language considered "politically binding" but not legally binding, and wear down the United States until it surrendered.

Bolton returned to D.C. but left behind his enormous team of negotiators from the various U.S. agencies. The United States also appointed three "public" members of the official delegation, all of whom understood the political implications of the proposed treaty: Congressman Bob Barr of Georgia, former Congressman Chip Pashayan of California, and former U.S. Ambassador to Switzerland Faith Whittlesey.

Still, the next ten days played out as a David and Goliath metaphor, with the United States alone in the position of fighting off the biased media, anti-gun delegations from countries such as Japan and Canada, and the relentless fervor of the hundreds of anti-gun NGOs represented at the conference.

Other nations that opposed elements of the treaty were

content to sit back and let the United States take the heat, knowing from Bolton's speech that the U.S. position was firm, and that they wouldn't have to get their own hands dirty. The central talking point of the global gun-ban elite was to claim that the United States had isolated itself against a global consensus to restrict firearms in a U.N. treaty. On Main Street, USA, this is a claim to glory. But in the hallways of the U.N. building, isolation was considered a major offense against the very concept of the U.N. itself.

Chip Pashayan later told NewsMax.com, "It was magnificent to see the U.S. stand up against these forces and not buckle under to what was international political pressure, which was very formidable notwithstanding the fact that the U.S. is the big boy on the block."

Second Amendment scholar David Kopel, who monitored the discussions, later wrote in *National Review*:

> *The U.S. delegation consistently rejected efforts at 'compromise,' which would have kept some anti-gun language in the treaty but made it softer and more ambiguous. An American delegation that was terrified of being "isolated" would have accepted the ambiguous language—on the theory that the Americans could later apply a pro-rights interpretation to the ambiguities. The Bush delegation was wiser: It recognized that, at the U.N., a conference final document is just the starting point. From there, U.N. bureaucrats will "monitor" how a country "complies" with such documents, and the bureaucrats resolving the ambiguities will favor their own radical agendas.*

The anti-gun delegates were befuddled. In the past, they had successfully worked together to wear down the United States in negotiating the specifics of other treaties. The U.S. negotiators were conditioned to moving their positions incrementally in the process, and checking back frequently with their bosses in Washington to see what they could live with. In his NewsMax interview, Pashayan noted, "The people from the State Department would have been more inclined to compromise to produce an agreement, that's their business. But they were prepared to follow the directions coming from above to stick with the 'redlines' and not go along with watered-down language."

Going completely against the grain of the soft and fuzzy consensus process, Bolton's speech had drawn a line in the sand. The United States team had no intention of allowing that line to be crossed, despite the relentless and growing pressure.

The standoff would last beyond the scheduled closing of the conference, forcing negotiators to go into an all-night bargaining session on the final night.

Delegates were huddled in Conference Room 4 of the U.N. General Assembly building. It was Friday, July 20— slated as the final day of the conference.

Tense negotiations had gone on late into the night on Thursday.

The major bones of contention had boiled down to two of the "redlines" established in Bolton's speech.

The U.S. team refused to budge on language to prohibit small arms exports to "non-state actors," an artful term coined by the diplomatic set to describe anyone who was not an official government recognized by the U.N. The American team rightly refused this language outright, noting that it would prohibit support for freedom fighters, people resisting tyrannical governments (such as our colonial minutemen at Lexington and Concord) or even long-time allies like Taiwan that are not formally recognized by the U.N. as a state.

The other redline was drawn over language to "seriously consider legal restrictions on unrestricted trade in and ownership of small arms and light weapons." In the alarmingly vague U.N. vernacular, this language amounted to a direct attack on the civilian ownership of firearms of any kind.

African nations were insisting on the "non-state actor" language, due in no small part to their desire to solidify and consolidate power behind their current governments, and stripping opposition forces of the means to challenge their authority.

Anti-gun delegates moved to preserve some shred of the language prohibiting civilian ownership. Conference president Camillo Reyes of Colombia attempted to mediate, proposing a compromise in which the language would be moved to the preamble of the document, where it would be perceived as having less force. At every impasse, Reyes complained about the Americans' stubborn refusal to entertain compromise, and ordered the conference to finish debate over some other, unresolved language irrelevant to the core negotiations.

It was by then Saturday morning, about 4 a.m., and the core dispute could be avoided no longer. Canadian negotiators introduced another watered-down version of the "non-state actor" language, which would say only that a nation "has to bear special responsibility when it would send arms to non-state actors." Canada dangled a package deal; if the U.S. would accept this vague statement, it would agree to deletion of the language on civilian ownership. Negotiators fell into silence as they realized that Canada had decided to push the United States to the edge of the envelope.

We said no.

Reyes again criticized the United States and ordered a break. Pashayan told NewsMax that some exhausted members of the negotiating team wanted to accept the Canadian compromise, although it, too, could hamper a future U.S. president in foreign policy. Drawing on more than a decade's experience as a congressman, Pashayan counseled a steady hand, suggesting that the U.S. simply refuse the deal and see what happened next.

Pashayan's counsel was correct. When the conference reconvened, the African nations dropped their demands. Following their lead, the developed nations opposing the U.S. position said they would follow the Africans' lead. As the sun rose over Manhattan, the final document was readied for consideration while the negotiators got a few hours sleep.

The document was consolidated into a single draft and headed with the title "Programme of Action." It would be considered "politically binding," meaning that it lacked legal authority but nonetheless represented the consensus of participating nations. It did not violate any of the American's stated redlines, at least not technically, and it allowed the opposition to salvage some "face" for the time and effort spent on negotiations. In sum, it was the perfect political deal—no one was particularly happy with it, it meant essentially nothing in terms of binding law, but it nonetheless allowed everyone involved to say they had "done something" about the problem, whether real or imagined.

U.S. negotiators were not pleased, however, that the final draft still contained a call for a follow-up conference in 2006. But it was too late for more discussions. Reyes quickly brought the final document up for consideration, and pronounced it passed by consensus. The delegates then proceeded to deliver a lengthy series of speeches congratulating Reyes for garnering approval, but expressing disappointment that the Americans had prevailed in negotiations.

> Pashayan summed up the experience for NewsMax:
> *This is not the end. This is the beginning skirmish of a war.... All of this has to be understood as part of a process leading ultimately to a treaty that will give an international body power over our domestic laws. That is why we must make sure that there is nothing, express or implied, that would give even the appearance of infringing on our Bill of Rights, which includes the Second Amendment."*

Of course, 2006 did come around—and with it another watershed victory in the history of U.N. gun control.

On the first day of the 2006 conference, U.N. Secretary General Kofi Annan claimed the Conference's purpose was not to ban "law abiding citizens right to bear arms...." However, others in the anti-gun cabal obviously disagreed. Indonesia's representative said, "We believe that no armed group outside of the State should be allowed to bear weapons." Bad news indeed for your local rifle team. Indonesia also suggested (in a manner reminiscent of anti-gun Sen. Daniel Patrick Moynihan's old comment that "guns don't kill people, bullets kill people") that "the issue of ammunition should also be addressed ... because in the absence of ammunition, small arms and light weapons pose no danger."

The next day, John Bolton's State Department successor, Under Secretary of State Robert Joseph, politely but forcefully gave the U.S. "red lines." These included interference with Americans' right to arms, a U.N. ban on transfer of arms to freedom fighters and international regulation of ammunition. The U.S. also said it was not ready to commit to any future conferences on small arms. As Joseph noted later:

> *The U.S. Constitution guarantees the rights of our citizens to keep and bear arms, and there will be no infringement of those rights.... The United States will not agree to any provisions restricting civilian possession, use or legal trade of firearms inconsistent with our laws and practices.*

Not until the third day did a new draft of the U.N. "Small Arms" Conference "final" report become public. Unfortunately, the draft contained provisions on two issues the U.S. would not accept—the ban on transfer of arms to freedom fighters and international regulation of ammunition. The proposed document also called for U.N. meetings on "small arms," including additional conferences in 2008, 2010, and 2012. Holding meetings is, of course, something the U.N. is good at—for international bureaucrats, it beats taking action on hard issues. The U.S., on the other hand, opposed holding yet more meetings to rehash the same issues.

Over the next few days, one anti-gun NGO after another made statements to the meeting. Mary Leigh Blek of the so-called "Million Mom March" made an emotional anti-gun speech to the delegates.

Fortunately, pro-gun groups also made presentations, pointing out that the U.N. had never disavowed any plans to interfere with lawful private gun ownership. As Dr. Carlo Peroni, president of the World Forum on the Future of Sport Shooting Activities (WFSA), put it, "We are always left with a nebulous 'trust us.'" C. Edward Rowe, chairman of WFSA's Manufacturer's Advisory Group, added that "it serves no real useful purpose for [the U.N.] to expend its effort on the lawfully owned civilian firearms of the world. ... [T]he 'net' must be designed so as to allow the legitimate to survive and to catch only the illicit."

Many international pro-gun representatives added the weight of their own countries' experiences. Hermann Suter of Switzerland's Pro Tell said it was "precisely because of our civilian armaments that in World War II our country went unplundered and we survived a terrible time in history in exactly that peace." Suter pointed out that with shooting ranges throughout the country and with active youth marksmanship programs, Switzerland is one of the safest countries in the world.

Pro-gun representatives also noted the safe and positive uses of firearms. As David Penn of the British Shooting Sports Council (BSSC) said, "The civilian ownership and use of firearms for hunting, wildlife management, target shooting or collecting are remarkably safe activities. I have had more frights in a couple of hours driving on a crowded British motorway than in a lifetime of being around firearms." And Rick Parsons of Safari Club International described the benefits of hunting for economic development, describing how "hunting programs have changed the lives of those widely recognized as the most disadvantaged and marginalized people in the world."

Most importantly, the pro-gun groups made clear that U.N. gun control schemes would inevitably fail. Canadian criminologist Gary Mauser pointed out that Canada's firearms registration system had failed to save lives, because "crime rates are driven by sociological factors … rather than availability of just one method of murder." Tony Bernardo of the Canadian Institute for Legislative Action echoed Mauser's comments and pointed out the political consequences of the Canadian gun registry; as Bernardo put it, "[t]he government that produced the programme is, shall we say, no longer with us."

Mauser pointed out that U.N. involvement in the gun issue could backfire against the U.N. in the same way, noting the "danger the UN will lose further trust and credibility around the globe, and ultimately take part in the prolongation of poverty, misery and the lack of prospect of entire peoples, by mistakenly directing its attention towards private gun ownership."

BSSC's Penn aptly summarized the views of the world's gun owners, pointing out that "The civilian firearms owner has a strong attachment to his or her guns, and, whatever you might think about such emotions, neither the shooter nor his firearms is about to go away."

The conference wore on, with innumerable speeches and little action. The President of the Conference,

Ambassador Kariyawasam from Sri Lanka, released another draft of the Conference report. The draft again pushed international regulation of ammunition and, of course, six more years of meetings.

Eventually, the conference came back to the issue of U.N. regulation of civilian firearms. That move was led by Mexico, Colombia, and, of all countries, Canada. Many observers were chagrined that the Canadian delegation would take such an anti-gun stand since there was a brand-new Conservative government in Ottawa. Canadian disarmament bureaucrats seemed to be running the delegation.

On the eighth—and next to last—day, delegates again agreed during an evening session, with some saying that if an agreement could not be reached, the Conference would be deadlocked. As the evening dragged on, the concept of U.N. regulation of civilian firearms seemed to refuse to die, even though the U.S. adamantly held the line on the issue.

NRA's team was vigilant—fearing a last-minute "breakthrough" that would bring about the U.N.'s beloved "consensus" on the issue.

Yet, this time, the truly unexpected happened: On the ninth and last day, the conference ended in a deadlock with no formal conclusions or recommendations—on anything. Perhaps most startling, given the U.N.'s obsession with process over substance, the delegates failed to agree even to meet again.

The collapse of the 2006 conference was a pivotal moment in the fight against global gun control. It showed that determined opposition by one government, and by defenders of the right to arms, can derail the best efforts of an entire global bureaucracy and its activist allies.

Yet the story isn't over. Anti-gun NGOs and governments plan to repackage their ideas in the guise of an "Arms Trade Treaty" (ATT). Led by the British, the effort for an "Arms Trade Treaty" would be the same spoiled wine in new bottles.

The movement for an "Arms Trade Treaty" started just a few months after the collapse of the July 2006 conference. On December 6th, the U.N. General Assembly voted to pass General Assembly Resolution 61/89, "Towards an arms trade treaty." The vote was 153-1 in favor of the resolution—with the United States standing alone. Almost as striking, there were 24 abstentions. The abstainers included both some of the major arms exporters to the Third World—such as China—and some of the despotic regimes whose subjects most desperately need the means to defend themselves—such as Sudan.

But the U.N. resolution ignores those needs. Instead, it suggests that the lack of arms control laws causes "conflict, the displacement of people, crime and terrorism," and therefore undermines "peace, reconciliation, safety, security, stability and sustainable development."

In classic U.N. fashion, the resolution calls for a series of studies—first by the Secretary-General, then by a "group of governmental experts"—on the feasibility of "a comprehensive, legally binding instrument establishing common international standards for the import, export and transfer of conventional arms." Leaving little doubt how the studies will come out, the General Assembly put the "Arms Trade Treaty" on its agenda for its next meeting.

Our opponents may decide, in the face of stiff U.S. resistance, not to seek changes in an "Arms Trade Treaty" but simply to try and make the 2001 "Programme" legally binding. So if there are no changes in the document itself, what impact could the existing document have on our rights?

The answer is—plenty. The language is vague and sweeping, and it doesn't take much imagination to see how the gun-ban crowd could insist on the most extreme reading of its elements. Here's a rundown of the major existing provisions agreed to by consensus in 2001, quoted directly from the document:

> *To put in place, where they do not exist, adequate laws, regulations and administrative procedures to exercise effective control over the production of SALW (small arms and light weapons) within their areas of jurisdiction, and over the export, import, transit or retransfer of such weapons.*

Read it again, and remember, there is no definition of "small arms and light weapons." Not to mention adequate laws, effective control, and transit or retransfer. Who decides what is adequate? Who defines "effective control"?

I do know the meaning of transit and retransfer, and these terms encompass merely traveling with firearms, or giving or selling firearms to friends or family, or buying a gun at a gun show.

> *Ensure that comprehensive and accurate records are kept for as long as possible on the manufacture, holding and transfer of SALW.*

Comprehensive and accurate records, kept as long as possible. The United States already does that for the manufacturing of firearms, but "holding and transfer" means possession and purchase.

This provision is code for a massive, international gun registration database, a deep pond for unlimited fishing expeditions by U.N. bureaucrats and investigators.

> *Develop adequate national legislation or administrative procedures regulating the activities of those who engage in SALW brokering.*

What is a gun dealer if not a broker between the manufacturer and customer?

And here again, what exactly is "adequate"? As the U.S. team realized during negotiations, the answers to these questions will come not from a dictionary or neutral party, but from U.N. bureaucrats who are already on record opposing our constitutional freedoms.

> *Ensure confiscated, seized or collected SALW are destroyed.*

Any Americans who aren't worried about firearms being confiscated have their heads in the sand. In 2005 we saw authorities going house to house in New Orleans after the Hurricane Katrina disaster, pounding on doors and illegally confiscating firearms. The National Rifle Association stopped them in court, and the judge ordered the confiscated guns returned, but if the U.N. has its way there would be nothing to return but scraps of metal and heaps of ashes.

> *Develop and implement, where possible, effective disarmament, demobilization, and reintegration*

programmes.

So after we are disarmed, the U.N. wants us demobilized and reintegrated. I can hear it now: "Step right this way for your reprogramming, sir. Once we confiscate your guns we can demobilize your aggressive instincts and reintegrate you into civil society."

No thanks.

Encourage regional negotiations with the aim of concluding relevant legally binding instruments aimed at preventing, combating and eradicating the illicit trade, and where they do exist to ratify and fully implement them.

The anti-gun forces are encouraging countries to use other multinational groups, such as the Organization of American States or the European Union, to negotiate stricter treaties, make them binding, and push them through to ratification. It's intended to open up other fronts of attack, and it has been successful, as you will learn.

Encourage the strengthening of moratoria or similar initiatives in affected regions or subregions on the transfer and manufacture of SALW.

This one is simple. "Moratoria" is the plural of moratorium, a fancy word for ban.

Finally, the real whopper:

Promote a dialogue and a culture of peace by encouraging education and public awareness programmes on the problems of the illicit trade in SALW.

Let's connect the dots here. SALW means our guns. Illicit trade, to many U.N. delegates, means any civilian trade whatsoever. So the "culture of peace" means no guns in civilian hands—a monopoly of force held by the state.

We don't need a dialogue about that concept; our Founders had a vigorous dialogue when they crafted the Bill of Rights to the U.S. Constitution. They expressly rejected a monopoly of force held by the state, and for good reason. But if the U.N. has its way, our cherished constitutional freedoms will be obliterated to reach the naïve fantasy of a "culture of peace."

I can hear some readers now, "Oh, Wayne's just overreacting. That's not what these people really want."

It is. And you don't have to take my word for it.

In 2004, I traveled to London to publicly debate Rebecca Peters, head of the International Action Network on Small Arms (IANSA). She is the chief of an umbrella group of NGOs, more than 500 of them, who are all working together toward a global gun ban. Debating before an audience at King's College, I was amazed at how openly Ms. Peters was willing to admit the long-term goals of their movement.

Peters quoted U.N. head Kofi Annan as saying, "The easy availability of small arms has contributed to violence and political insecurity, and have [sic] imperiled human security in every way." She told the audience that,

"Guns are involved in human rights abuses . . . guns obstruct peacekeeping activities . . . guns hinder development, investment, and tourism."

That's a long indictment! But she was just getting started.

"Guns don't respect borders," she continued, citing

the same argument of our national gun-ban groups when they complain about "lax" gun laws in our rural states causing crime in major cities. "There is a patchwork of laws globally," she started, echoing another canard of our domestic debate.

And she grabbed one last arrow from the rhetorical quiver of the U.S. gun ban lobby, claiming that increased crime rates in Britain were due not to their gun bans, but the "loophole" of failing to ban airguns and replicas.

And then she told the group that the Programme of Action represented only "moderate measures" to "reform" gun laws globally. She stated that the U.N.'s efforts to pass a gun-ban treaty represented "civil society saying stop!" to the United States.

It became clear that in Peters's view, our guns were equivalent to military ordnance and weapons of mass destruction. "Treaties are how we deal with nuclear, chemical and biological weapons," she said, "only guns are exempt." She vented her wrath on the United States, saying, "The U.S. should recognize it's not exempt from the world, contributes disproportionately to world problems, and should cooperate."

An audience member pointed out that the U.S. Constitution prevented her vision of "cooperation" with the gun-ban treaty, but she persisted, complaining that the U.S. position represented the attitude that American citizens are "more equal than others."

Peters detailed the starting point of the "moderate reforms" she wanted the U.N. to ram down the throat of America's law-abiding citizens: "owner licensing, registration, certain categories of guns should not be available, and limits on the number of guns civilians can own. Her goal, she claimed, was to "keep guns out of the hands of people who are irresponsible." When asked who that might be, she shrugged, saying that "good people sometimes do bad things" and that lawful self-defense "only happens in the movies."

I told the audience that if Peters and the U.N. couldn't tell the bad people from the good, we were all going to be in a lot of trouble. The audience pressed Peters for more detail on what type of firearms Americans should be allowed to own.

Peters responded, "I think American citizens shouldn't be exempt from the rules that apply to the rest of the world. ... Americans should have only guns suitable for purposes they can prove."

An audience member told Peters his target shooting guns had been confiscated, and asked if this disturbed her in any way. She responded, "Countries change, laws change, why are firearms exempt? The definition of sporting activity is always under pressure. Target shooting is not a legitimate sport! If you miss your sport, take up another!"

Now the audience was riled, and Peters was flustered when she delivered her closing remarks, saying: "Guns cause enormous suffering in the world at large. So much for guns and freedom. The U.S. is the country with the largest proportion of its population in prison ... we should be talking about prevention. People have a right to live free from fear. Wayne has been watching too many movies. Common sense dictates that guns do not make people or societies safer."

The audience had grown skeptical, and I tried to put her words in a larger perspective. I told the crowd that we saw the IANSA mission for what it was—the reemergence of the same old socialist fantasies of the twentieth century—fantasies that prey on citizens who fall for the false promise of social engineering. I described the global gun-ban forces as elitists who think they know better than us how to live our lives, spend our money, educate our children, and protect our homes. They are people who believe that if they could just be in charge, they could make our lives perfect. Their basic premise now is that if you will surrender your right to own a firearm to the whims of a new global bureaucracy, you will be safe. But I counseled the audience to study the history of nations where the social engineers have had their way, and suggested they should think twice about the bargain.

Americans simply won't fall for it, I explained. We are the freest nation in the world, and the false promise of the social engineers is precisely the bargain rejected by our forefathers.

I explained why Peters's vision was so frightening to Americans. Her vision is sweeping international police powers, offensive to every notion of our Bill of Rights. I told the audience to look at her own words, papers, and testimony, and they would find endless demands for recordkeeping, oversight, inspections, supervision, tracking, tracing, surveillance, marking, verification, paper trails, and databases.

And I pointed out that—no matter Peters' lofty words and noble rhetoric—nowhere in her documents would you find any provision by which oppressed people would be liberated or freed from dictatorship. Nowhere in her work is there a thought about respecting the right to self-defense, privacy, property, due process, or political freedom of any kind.

I closed by asking the audience to join the fight for freedom—because these competing visions will clash again.

IANSA and the global gun-ban forces have spent the years since the first conference opening new fronts for the clash of competing visions, and each one poses a unique threat to our freedoms. Each is also intended to add to the growing global clamor for the U.S. to surrender its principled stand on the private ownership of firearms.

In October 2005, two other major international groups pushed forward for new restrictions on small arms. At an October 3 meeting in Luxembourg, foreign ministers of the European Union "backed demands for a new international treaty on the arms trade to outlaw tracking in small arms," according to an article in *Defense News*. Proposed by Great Britain's foreign secretary Jack Straw, the statement was greeted gleefully by global gun-ban groups. Simon Grey, the arms control campaign manager at NGO Oxfam, "hailed the decision as a 'massive step toward stricter' controls on firearms.

A hemisphere away, in our nation's capital, the Organization of American States (OAS) held a two-day meeting "aimed at developing steps to prevent and combat illicit arms trafficking in the Western Hemisphere," according to a press release from our very own Department of State. The assistant secretary-general of the OAS called the arms trade a "transnational scourge," and said its effect on society "ranks among the most disastrous criminal activities against humankind." The meeting was led by a delegate from Colombia and held in accordance with the OAS "Inter-American Convention Against the Illicit

Manufacturing and Trafficking in Firearms, Ammunition, Explosives, and Other Related Materials." In the press release, the Colombian delegate called the convention "'groundbreaking and unique' as it is the first binding legal agreement on this issue."

Wait a minute. Isn't this the same "legally binding" concept we're fighting at the U.N.? And why did you never hear about the Senate approving this treaty?

Because it never has. The OAS treaty was first proposed in 1998, during the Clinton years. Since then, the career State Department bureaucrats have pushed for Senate ratification of the proposed OAS treaty, but the Foreign Relations Committee has never taken it up.

But instead of stopping the process, the Senate's considerable delay only inspired the bureaucrats to seek an avenue of less resistance. They recast the proposed treaty as a mere "convention," not requiring Senate approval.

The bureaucrats are surely proud of their work. In the press release, they stated that "the entry into force in 1998 of the Inter-American convention against illicit arms trafficking made the OAS a leader in multilateral efforts to address the problem of illicit weapons trafficking." How did the "entry into force" happen without Senate approval? The press release states, "The United States is a signatory to the convention and supports efforts to 'aggressively' implement its provisions."

So now we have treaties that don't require Senate ratification, by merely making the United States a "signatory" to a "convention" instead. So much for checks and balances.

The clash of competing visions is not limited to the United States versus the global gun-ban groups. In the midst are career bureaucrats, both here and abroad, whose jobs depend on negotiating agreements, not making principled stands. They are pushing forward on multiple fronts, out of the public eye, and seemingly without supervision.

This is their business, and we are newcomers to the process, vastly outnumbered by their legions. They are operating in venues that didn't even exist a few short years ago. They are supported by the global media and reinforced by the work of thousands of paid NGO staffers who are dedicated solely to moving a global gun ban forward. We are vastly under funded compared to the billions of dollars received by NGOs in "international aid and development" grants, some of which originate in our very own tax coffers. There are times when I wonder whether it's even possible to beat them at their own game.

But then I am reminded that this debate is not about process, policy, or global politics. At its core, this debate is about people, and the value we place on freedom.

Another development in October 2005 reminded me of freedom's enduring appeal. Social engineers in Brazil placed a binding gun-ban question on the national ballot for the October 23 elections. With majority support, the ballot question would completely outlaw the sale of firearms and ammunition to private citizens. Rebecca Peters awaited the results of the vote on the edge of her seat, telling *The Nation*, "If it passes, the referendum will show other countries that the gun lobby can be beaten. If that happens, we believe campaigns will arise in other countries, in Latin American and elsewhere, for a moratorium, or for serious restrictions, on the proliferation of guns." There's their favorite word for ban again, "moratorium."

And now she's talking about "serious" restrictions,

not just the "moderate" ones she outlined in our debate. No wonder she was so excited at the prospect of a national vote in Brazil to ban guns.

On the day of the vote, voters stood in long lines to cast their ballots—voting is mandatory in Brazil, punishable by a fine. Political observers predicted the ban would pass by a landslide. And at the end of the day, however, the referendum was rejected by a vote of nearly 65 percent.

Freedom's enduring appeal had triumphed again.

But not for long.

Despite all the pundits who said the referendum would set a global precedent, Brazil's gun-ban groups vowed to try again. The vaunted "will of the people" only seems to count when the people agree with the gun-ban agenda. "This closes the issue now, but maybe the next generation will be able to have this discussion again," said a local leader of the gun-ban campaign. "I hope the whole world will be able to deal with this again."

In the years to come, freedom will face its fiercest challenge yet, from the concerted forces of the global gun-ban corps who have spent the years since 2001 gearing up for their second bite at the apple—a second attempt to destroy the freedoms that are as American as apple pie.

The U.N., which recently celebrated its sixtieth anniversary, was founded with the highest hopes to promote peace among the world's nations and human rights for the world's peoples. Yet when it comes to both its peacekeeping and human rights missions the U.N. has proven itself utterly bankrupt. *The Economist* recently brought this manifest failure into sharp relief in an editorial focusing on the U.N.'s disgraceful 53-member Commission on Human Rights. *The Economist* pointed out that the Commission "is packed with members who are themselves serial abusers of human rights." It called Zimbabwe, Sudan, China, Cuba, Saudi Arabia, Nepal, and Russia "a veritable roll call of the worst offenders."

Add to this the almost daily reports in the media of U.N. corruption, including what can only be described as a "culture of rape" among U.N. peacekeepers around the world. Decent men and women, not only in America but worldwide, must vigorously oppose U.N. attempts to disarm civilian populations—especially those in dire need of the tools for self defense.

Not long after the United Nations was founded, Sir Winston Churchill offered the following about the new world body: "We must make sure that its work is fruitful, that it is a reality and not a sham, that it is a true temple of peace in which the shields of many nations can some day be hung up, and not merely a cockpit in a Tower of Babel."

When this great leader said "we," he was really speaking of you and me.

What would he say today?

APPENDIX A:
Guarantees Of The Right To Arms In State Constitutions

Alabama
That the great, general and essential principles of liberty and free government may be recognized and established, we declare.... That every citizen has a right to bear arms in defense of himself and the state. (Art. I, § 26) (1819)

Alaska
A well-regulated militia being necessary to the security of a free state, the right of the people to keep and bear arms shall not be infringed. The individual right to keep and bear arms shall not be denied or infringed by the State or a political subdivision of the State. (Art. I, § 19) (1994; previous version 1959)

Arizona
The right of the individual citizen to bear arms in defense of himself or the State shall not be impaired, but nothing in this section shall be construed as authorizing individuals or corporations to organize, maintain or employ an armed body of men. (Art. II, § 26) (1912)

Arkansas
The citizens of this State shall have the right to keep and bear arms for their common defense. (Art. II, § 5) (1868; previous versions 1864, 1861, 1836)

Colorado

The right of no person to keep and bear arms in defense of his home, person and property, or in aid of the civil power when thereto legally summoned, shall be called in question; but nothing herein contained shall be construed to justify the practice of carrying concealed weapons. (Art. II, § 13) (1876)

Connecticut

Every citizen has a right to bear arms in defense of himself and the state. (Art. I, § 15) (1818)

Delaware

A person has the right to keep and bear arms for the defense of self, family, home and State, and for hunting and recreational use. (Art. I, § 20) (1987)

Florida

The right of the people to keep and bear arms in defense of themselves and of the lawful authority of the state shall not be infringed, except that the manner of bearing arms may be regulated by law. (Art. I, § 8, [a]) (1990; previous versions 1968, 1885, 1868, 1838)

Georgia

The right of the people to keep and bear arms shall not be infringed, but the General Assembly shall have the power to prescribe the manner in which arms may be borne. (1982 Constitution, Art. I, § 1, para. 8) (1982; previous versions 1877, 1868, 1865)

Hawaii

A well regulated militia being necessary to the security of a free state, the right of the people to keep and bear arms shall not be infringed. (Art. I, § 15) (1959)

Idaho

The people have the right to keep and bear arms, which right shall not be abridged; but this provision shall not prevent the passage of laws to govern the carrying of weapons concealed on the person nor prevent passage of legislation providing minimum sentences for crimes committed while in possession of a firearm, nor prevent passage of legislation providing penalties for the possession of firearms by a convicted felon, nor prevent the passage of legislation punishing the use of a firearm. No law shall impose licensure, registration or special taxation on the ownership or possession of firearms or ammunition. Nor shall any law permit the confiscation of firearms, except those actually used in the commission of a felony. (Art. I, § 11) (1978; previous version 1889)

Illinois

Subject only to the police power, the right of the individual citizen to keep and bear arms shall not be infringed. (Art. I, § 22) (1970)

Indiana

The people shall have a right to bear arms, for the defense of themselves and the State. (Art. I, § 32) (1851; previous version, 1816)

Kansas

The people have the right to bear arms for their defense and security; but standing armies, in time of peace, are dangerous to liberty, and shall not be tolerated, and the military shall be in strict subordination to the civil power. (Bill of Rights, § 4) (1859)

Kentucky

All men are, by nature, free and equal, and have certain inherent and inalienable rights, among which may be reckoned: ... [t]he right to bear arms in defense of themselves and of the state, subject to the power of the general assembly to enact laws to prevent persons from carrying concealed weapons. (Bill of Rights, § 1) (1891; previous versions 1850, 1799)

Louisiana

The right of each citizen to keep and bear arms shall not be abridged, but this provision shall not prevent the passage of laws to prohibit the carrying of weapons concealed on the person. (Art. I, § 11) (1974; previous version 1879)

Maine

Every person has a right to keep and bear arms and this right shall never be questioned. (Art. I, § 16)(1987; previous version 1819)

Massachusetts

The people have a right to keep and bear arms for the common defence. And as, in time of peace, armies are dangerous to liberty, they ought not to be maintained without the consent of the legislature; and the military power shall always be held in an exact subordination to the civil authority, and be governed by it. (Part I, Art. XVII) (1780)

Michigan

Every person has a right to keep or bear arms for the defense of himself and the State. (Art. I, § 6) (1963; previous versions 1850, 1835)

Mississippi

The right of every citizen to keep and bear arms in defense of his home, person, or property, or in aid of the civil power when thereto legally summoned, shall not be called in question, but the legislature may regulate or forbid carrying concealed weapons. (Art. III, § 12) (1890; previous versions 1868, 1817)

Missouri

That the right of every citizen to keep and bear arms in defense of his home, person, and property, or when lawfully summoned in aid of the civil power, shall not be questioned; but this shall not justify the wearing of concealed weapons. (Art. I, § 23) (1945; previous versions 1875, 1865, 1820)

Montana
The right of any person to keep or bear arms in defense of his own home, person, and property, or in aid of the civil power when thereto legally summoned, shall not be called in question; but nothing herein contained shall be held to permit the carrying of concealed weapons. (Art. II, § 12) "Militia forces shall consist of all able-bodied citizens of the state except those excepted by law." (Art. VI, § 14)(1889)

Nebraska
All persons are by nature free and independent, and have certain inherent and inalienable rights; among these are life, liberty, the pursuit of happiness, and the right to keep and bear arms for security or defense of self, family, home and others, and for lawful common defense, hunting, recreational use and all other lawful purposes, and such rights shall not be denied or infringed by the state or any subdivision thereof. (Art. I, § 1) (1988)

Nevada
Every citizen has the right to keep and bear arms for security and defense, for lawful hunting and recreational use and for other lawful purposes. (Art. I, § 11, [1]) (1982)

New Hampshire
All persons have the right to keep and bear arms in defense of themselves, their families, their property and the state. (Part I, Art. 2a) No person, who is conscientiously scrupulous about the lawfulness of bearing arms, shall be compelled thereto. (Part I, Art. 13) (1982)

New Mexico

No law shall abridge the right of the citizen to keep and bear arms for security and defense, for lawful hunting and recreational use and for other lawful purposes, but nothing herein shall be held to permit the carrying of concealed weapons. No municipality or county shall regulate in any way, an incident of the right to keep and bear arms. (Art. II, § 6) (1986; previous versions 1971, 1912)

North Carolina

A well regulated militia being necessary to the security of a free State, the right of the people to keep and bear arms shall not be infringed; and, as standing armies in time of peace are dangerous to liberty, they shall not be maintained, and the military shall be kept under strict subordination to, and governed by, the civil power. Nothing herein shall justify the practice of carrying concealed weapons, or prevent the General Assembly from enacting penal statutes against that practice. (Art. I, § 30) (1971; previous versions 1876, 1868, 1776)

North Dakota

All individuals are by nature equally free and independent and have certain inalienable rights, among which are those of enjoying and defending life and liberty; acquiring, possessing and protecting property and reputation; pursuing and obtaining safety and happiness; and to keep and bear arms for the defense of their person, family, property, and the state, and for lawful hunting, recreational and other lawful purposes, which shall not be infringed. (Art. I, § 1) (1984)

Ohio
The people have the right to bear arms for their defense and security; but standing armies, in time of peace, are dangerous to liberty, and shall not be kept up; and the military shall be in strict subordination to the civil power. (Art. I, §4) (1851; previous version 1802)

Oklahoma
The right of a citizen to keep and bear arms in defense of his home, person or property, or in aid of the civil power, when thereunto legally summoned, shall never be prohibited; but nothing herein contained shall prevent the Legislature from regulating the carrying of weapons. (Art. II, § 26) (1907)

Oregon
The people shall have the right to bear arms for the defence of themselves, and the State, but the Military shall be kept in strict subordination to the civil power. (Art. I, § 27) (1857)

Pennsylvania
The right of the citizens to bear arms in defence of themselves and the State shall not be questioned. (Art. I, § 21) (1790)

Rhode Island
The right of the people to keep and bear arms shall not be infringed. (Art. I, § 22) (1842)

South Carolina
A well regulated militia being necessary to the security of a free State, the right of the people to keep and bear arms shall not be infringed. As, in times of peace, armies are dangerous to liberty, they shall not be maintained without the consent of the General Assembly. The military power of the State shall always be held in subordination to the civil authority and be governed by it. No soldier shall in time of peace be quartered in any house without the consent of the owner nor in time of war but in the manner prescribed by law. (Art. I, § 20) (1895; previous version 1868)

South Dakota
The right of the citizens to bear arms in defense of themselves and the state shall not be denied. (Art. VI, §24) (1889)

Tennessee
That the citizens of this State have a right to keep and bear arms for their common defense; but the Legislature shall have power, by law, to regulate the wearing of arms with a view to prevent crime. (Art. I, § 26) (1870; previous versions 1834, 1796)

Texas
Every citizen shall have the right to keep and bear arms in lawful defense of himself or the State; but the Legislature shall have power, by law, to regulate the wearing of arms, with a view to prevent crime. (Art. I, § 23) (1876; previous versions 1868, 1845)

Note: The Texas Declaration of Independence stated that "[The Mexican government] has demanded us to deliver up our arms, which are essential to our defense—the rightful property of freemen—and formidable only to tyrannical governments." The Republic of Texas Constitution of 1836 also protected Texans' right to arms.

Utah
The individual right of the people to keep and bear arms for security and defense of self, family, others, property, or the state as well as for other lawful purposes shall not be infringed; but nothing herein shall prevent the legislature from defining the lawful use of arms. (Art. I, § 6) (1984; previous version 1895)

Vermont
That the people have a right to bear arms for the defence of themselves and the State—and as standing armies in time of peace are dangerous to liberty, they ought not to be kept up; and that the military should be kept under strict subordination to and governed by the civil power. (Chapter I, Art. 16) (1777)

Virginia
That a well regulated militia, composed of the body of the people, trained to arms, is the proper, natural and safe defense of a free state, therefore, the right of the people to keep and bear arms shall not be infringed; that standing armies, in time of peace, should be avoided as dangerous to liberty; and that in all cases the military should be under strict subordination to, and governed by, the civil power. (Art. I, § 13) (1971; previous version 1776)

Washington

The right of the individual citizen to bear arms in defense of himself, or the state, shall not be impaired, but nothing in this section shall be construed as authorizing individuals or corporations to organize, maintain or employ an armed body of men. (Art. I, § 24) (1889)

West Virginia

A person has the right to keep and bear arms for the defense of self, family, home, and state, and for lawful hunting and recreational use. (Art. 3, § 22) (1986)

Wisconsin

The people have the right to keep and bear arms for security, defense, hunting, recreation, or any other lawful purpose. (Art. 1, § 25) (1998; approved by a 3:1 margin among Wisconsin voters)

Wyoming

The right of the citizens to bear arms in defense of themselves and of the state shall not be denied. (Art. I, § 24) (1889)

Notes:

California, Iowa, Maryland, Minnesota, New Jersey, and New York do not have "right to keep and bear arms" amendments in their state constitutions.

Iowa's constitution (Art. I, § 1) states: All men are, by nature, free and equal, and have certain inalienable rights—among which are those of enjoying and defending life and liberty, acquiring, possessing and protecting property, and pursuing and obtaining safety and happiness.

New Jersey's (Art. I, § 1) states: All persons are by nature free and independent, and have certain natural and unalienable rights, among which are those of enjoying and defending life and liberty, of acquiring, possessing, and protecting property, and of pursuing and obtaining safety, and happiness.

APPENDIX B:
Federal Court Cases Relating To The Second Amendment

U.S. Supreme Court Cases

***United States v. Cruikshank*, 92 U.S. 542 (1876).**
Defendants, members of the Ku Klux Klan, had been charged with, among other things, banding together, with intent "unlawfully and feloniously to injure, oppress, threaten, and intimidate" two citizens of the United States "of African descent and persons of color," with the unlawful and felonious intention of preventing them from exercising "the right to keep and bear arms for a lawful purpose" and other rights protected by the Bill of Rights.

The Court recognized that the right to keep and bear arms preexisted the Constitution (clearly implying that it is a right of individuals), but ruled that the Second Amendment protects it against acts of Congress, not against the actions of individuals. The Court declared:

> *The right there specified is that of "bearing arms for a lawful purpose." This is not a right granted by the Constitution. Neither is it in any manner dependent upon that instrument for its existence. The second amendment declares that it shall not be infringed; but this, as has been seen, means no more than that it shall not be infringed by Congress.*

***Presser v. Illinois*, 116 U.S. 252 (1886).** Presser was charged with violating an Illinois law, by parading in Chicago in an "unauthorized body of men with arms, who had associated themselves together as a military company and organization, without having a license from the Governor, and not being a part of, or belonging to, 'the regular organized volunteer militia' of the State of Illinois, or the troops of the United States."

The Court recognized, in several ways, that the right to keep and bear arms is a right of individuals. It cited the *Cruikshank* decision's statement that the right to arms preexisted the Constitution, it did not reject Presser's appeal for lack of Second Amendment standing (and would have, if it had considered the right to arms something other than a right of individuals), and it identified the militia (referred to in the Second Amendment) in broad terms:

> *It is undoubtedly true that all citizens capable of bearing arms constitute the reserved military force or reserve militia of the United States as well as of the States.... [T]he States cannot, even laying [the Second Amendment] out of view, prohibit the people from keeping and bearing arms, as so to deprive the United States of their rightful resource for maintaining the public security and disable the people from performing their duty to the general government.*

The Court ruled that the Illinois law in question did not violate the Second Amendment:

> *We think it clear that the sections under consideration, which only forbid bodies of men to associate together*

*as military organizations, or to drill or parade with
arms in cities and towns unless authorized by law, do
not infringe the right of the people to keep and bear
arms.... The right voluntarily to associate together
as a military company or organization, or to drill or
parade with arms, without, and independent of, an act
of Congress or law of the State authorizing the same,
is not an attribute of national citizenship.*

***Miller v. Texas*, 153 U.S. 535 (1894).** Miller
challenged a Texas statute, which prohibited the bearing of
pistols, as violative of the Second, Fourth and Fourteenth
Amendments, but did so for the first time after a state
appellate court had affirmed his conviction. Reiterating
Cruikshank and *Presser*, the Court first found that the
Second and Fourth Amendments, of themselves, did not
limit state action. The Court then turned to the claim
that the Texas statute violated the right to bear arms
and against warrantless searches as incorporated in the
Fourteenth Amendment. But because the Court would not
hear objections not made in a timely fashion, the Court
refused to consider Miller's contentions.

The Court confirmed that it had never addressed
the issue of the Second Amendment applying to the
states through the Fourteenth Amendment, but left open
the possibility that the right to arms, and freedom from
warrantless searches, would apply to the states through the
Fourteenth Amendment. (Since then, the Supreme Court
has held that the right to be secure against unreasonable
search and seizure, like nearly all provisions of the Bill
of Rights, does apply to the states through the Fourteenth
Amendment.)

***United States v. Miller*, 307 U.S. 174 (1939).** At trial, the defendants, who had been convicted of possessing a short-barreled shotgun not registered as required by the National Firearms Act, obtained a summary judgment striking down the NFA as a violation of the Second Amendment. The government appealed to the Supreme Court. Before the Court, the defendants and their lawyer were not present. Having no evidence from the defense to consider, the Court, citing *Aymette v. State*, 21 Tenn. 154 (1840), concluded:

> *The Court cannot take judicial notice that a shotgun having a barrel less than 18 inches long has today any reasonable relation to the preservation or efficiency of a well regulated militia; and therefore cannot say that the Second Amendment guarantees to the citizen the right to keep and bear such a weapon ... In the absence of any evidence tending to show that possession or use of a "shotgun having a barrel of less that eighteen inches in length" at this time has some reasonable relationship to the preservation or efficiency of a well regulated militia, we cannot say that the Second Amendment guarantees the right to keep and bear such an instrument. [The Court remanded the case to the trial court, to gather evidence on whether the shotgun had a relationship to the militia.]*

The Court stated that the amendment's purpose relates to the militia, which it recognized as consisting of able-bodied males of age, possessing privately-owned arms, a clear recognition that the right to arms is an individual right:

With obvious purpose to assure the continuation and render possible the effectiveness of [the Militia] the declaration and guarantee of the Second Amendment were made. It must be interpreted and applied with that end in view.... The signification attributed to the term Militia appears from the debates in the Convention, the history and legislation of Colonies and States, and the writings of approved commentators. These show plainly enough that the Militia comprised all males physically capable of acting in concert for the common defense. "A body of citizens enrolled for military discipline." And further, that ordinarily when called for service these men were expected to appear bearing arms supplied by themselves and of the kind in common use at the time.

Had the Court considered the Second Amendment to guarantee only a right to possess arms during active service in a select militia, or a "right" of a state to maintain a militia, it would have noted that the defendants were mere individuals, not active-duty militiamen or states.

***Lewis v. United States*, 445 U.S. 95 (1980).** The case was concerned only with whether the federal law that prohibits the possession of firearms by convicted felons violated the Second Amendment.

Since convicted felons have always been subject to the loss of numerous fundamental rights of citizenship, including the right to vote, hold office, and serve on juries, the Court concluded that laws prohibiting the possession of firearms by a convicted felon "are neither based upon constitutionally suspect criteria, nor do they trench upon any constitutionally protected liberties."

The Court paraphrased *U.S. v. Miller*, stating, "[T]he Second Amendment guarantees no right to keep and bear a firearm that does not have 'some reasonable relationship to the preservation or efficiency of a well-regulated militia.'"

***United States v. Verdugo-Urquidez*, 494 U.S. 259 (1990).** This case concerned the meaning of the term "the people" in the Fourth Amendment. Though the decision in the case was not unanimous, due to dissent over some issues, all nine justices recognized that the right to keep and bear arms is an individual right possessed by "the people":

> *"[T]he people" seems to have been a term of art employed in select parts of the Constitution. The Preamble declares that the Constitution is ordained and established by "the People of the United States." The Second Amendment protects "the right of the people to keep and bear Arms," and the Ninth and Tenth Amendments provide that certain rights and powers are retained by and reserved to "the people." See also U.S. Const. Amdt. 1, ("Congress shall make no law...abridging...the right of the people peaceably to assemble"); Art. 1, Sect. 2, cl. 1 ("The House of Representatives shall be composed of Members chosen every second Year by the people of the several states") While this textual exegesis is by no means conclusive, it suggests that "the people" protected by the Fourth Amendment, and by the First and Second Amendments, and to whom rights and powers are reserved in the Ninth and Tenth Amendments, refers to a class of persons who are a part of a national*

community or who have otherwise developed sufficient connection with this country to be considered part of that community.

U.S. Courts of Appeals Cases

United States v. Tot, **131 F.2d 261 (3d Cir. 1942), rev'd on other grounds, 319 U.S. 463 (1943).** Tot was a felon, convicted of possessing a .32 caliber pistol. One of Tot's challenges to the conviction was on Second Amendment grounds. The court held that prohibiting firearm possession by a convicted felon "is entirely reasonable and does not infringe upon the preservation of the well regulated militia protected by the Second Amendment."

The court also assumed that a .32 caliber pistol would not be protected by the Second Amendment under the *Miller* decision's reference to arms that have a "relationship to the preservation or efficiency of a well regulated militia."

The court also falsely stated that the Second Amendment's history indicated that it was intended to protect some sort of "collective right":

It is abundantly clear both from the discussions of this amendment contemporaneous with its proposal and adoption and those of learned writers since that this amendment, unlike those providing for protection of free speech and freedom of religion, was not adopted with individual rights in mind, but as a protection for the States in the maintenance of their militia organizations against possible encroachments by the federal power.

To the contrary, each of the 18th century "discussions" the Third Circuit cited dealt only with the desire of Anti-Federalists for constitutional constraints on the federal government's power to keep standing armies during peacetime, and strong guarantees of the states' ability to defend themselves militarily against a potentially tyrannical federal government.

> *The Third Circuit assumed that the Second Amendment was intended to erect "a protection for the States in the maintenance of their militia organizations against possible encroachment by the federal power." This assumption is demonstrably false—both as a matter of history, and because it entails the absurd assumption that the Second Amendment repealed the provisions in Article I of the Constitution that give the federal government control of the militia, and that forbid the states from keeping troops without the consent of Congress.*

***Cases v. United States*, 131 F.2d 916 (1st Cir. 1942), cert. denied sub nom. *Velazquez v. U. S.*, 319 U.S. 770 (1943).** In this case, the court held that the Supreme Court in *Miller* had not intended "to formulate a general rule" regarding which arms were protected by the Second Amendment and concluded, therefore, that many types of arms were not protected. Nonetheless, the court in *Cases* expressly acknowledged that the Second Amendment guarantees an individual right when it noted that the law in question "undoubtedly curtails to some extent the right of individuals to keep and bear arms...."

***Stevens v. United States*, 440 F.2d 144 (6th Cir. 1971).** This case involved possession of firearms by convicted felons. In a one-sentence holding, the court concluded that the Second Amendment "applies only to the right of the State to maintain a militia and not to the individual's right to bear arms...." The Court undertook no analysis of the history of the ratification of the Second Amendment, nor of *Miller*, merely citing the case as authority for its conclusion.

United States v. Decker, 446 F.2d 164 (8th Cir. 1971). As in the later *Synnes* case (below), the Eighth Circuit held that the defendant could present "evidence indicating a conflict" between the statute at issue and the Second Amendment. Since he failed to do so, the court declined to hold that the record-keeping requirements of the Gun Control Act of 1968 violated the Second Amendment. As in *Synnes*, the court implicitly recognized that the right guaranteed belonged to individuals.

United States v. Johnson, 441 F.2d 1134 (5th Cir. 1971). This decision quoted *U.S. v. Miller's* statement concerning the relationship of arms to the militia and rejected, without analysis, the defendant's challenge to the constitutionality of the National Firearms Act. The defendant failed to present evidence that the firearm in question had a relationship to the militia.

United States v. McCutcheon, 446 F.2d 133 (7th Cir. 1971). The court followed *Miller* in holding that the National Firearms Act did not infringe the Second Amendment.

United States v. Synnes, **438 F.2d 764 (8th Cir. 1971), vacated on other grounds, 404 U.S. 1009 (1972).** The court held that the federal law prohibiting possession of a firearm by a convicted felon did not infringe the Second Amendment. As there was "no showing that prohibiting possession of firearms by felons obstructs the maintenance of a 'well regulated militia,'" the court saw "no conflict" between the law and the Second Amendment.

United States v. Cody, **460 F.2d 34 (8th Cir. 1972).** After citing *Miller* for the propositions that "the Second Amendment is not an absolute bar to congressional regulation of the use or possession of firearms" and that the "Second Amendment's guarantee extends only to use or possession which 'has some reasonable relationship to the preservation or efficiency of a well-regulated militia,'" the court held that there was "no evidence that the prohibition of the federal prohibition on possession of a firearm by a felon obstructs the maintenance of a well-regulated militia."

United States v. Day, **476 F.2d 562 (6th Cir. 1973)**. This case involved possession of a firearm by persons dishonorably discharged from the Armed Forces, a violation of federal law. Citing *Miller*, the court merely concluded "there is no absolute right of an individual to possess a firearm." In so saying, the court implicitly recognized the individual right to possess firearms.

United States v. Johnson, **497 F.2d 548 (4th Cir. 1974).** At issue was the interstate transportation of a firearm by convicted felons, a violation of federal law. The court stated that the Second Amendment "only confers a collective right of keeping and bearing arms which must bear a 'reasonable relationship to the preservation or efficiency of a well-regulated militia.'"

As authority for that statement, the court cited *Miller* and *Cody v. United States*. Yet, as the Supreme Court in *Lewis* made clear, *Miller* held that it is the firearm itself, not the act of keeping and bearing the firearm, which must have a "reasonable relationship to the preservation or efficiency of a well-regulated militia."

United States v. Swinton, 521 F.2d 1255 (10th Cir. 1975). In the context of interpreting the meaning of the phrase "engaging in the business of dealing in firearms" (18 U.S.C. 922(a)(1)), the court noted, in dicta, that "there is no absolute constitutional right of an individual to possess a firearm." Clearly, therefore, the court recognized that the right is an individual one, though not absolute.

United States v. Warin, 530 F.2d 103 (6th Cir. 1976), cert. denied, 426 U.S. 948 (1976). Relying upon its decision in *Stevens*, the court concluded, without reference to the history of the Second Amendment, that it "is clear the Second Amendment guarantees a collective rather than an individual right." The court also indicated it relied on the First Circuit's decision in *Cases*. Yet in concluding that not all arms were protected by the Second Amendment, *Cases* did not hold, as *Warin* did, that the Second Amendment afforded individuals no protections whatever.

The court erred in concluding that Warin's relationship to the militia was relevant to determining whether his possession of a machine gun was protected by the Second Amendment since, in Miller, the Supreme Court focused on the firearm itself, not the individual involved.

United States v. Graves, 554 F.2d 65 (3rd Cir. 1977). Since the defendant in this case did not raise the Second Amendment as a challenge to the "statutory program which restricts the right to bear arms of convicted felons and other persons of dangerous propensities," the only discussion of the Second Amendment is found in a footnote wherein the court states "[a]rguably, any regulation of firearms may be violative of this constitutional provision."

United States v. Oakes, 564 F.2d 384 (10th Cir. 1977), cert. denied, 435 U.S. 926 (1978). This case involved a defendant who possessed an unregistered machine gun. The court implicitly recognized that the right to arms is an individual right, irrespective of the defendant's militia status. The court instead focused on whether the firearm in question had a relationship to the militia as outlined in *Miller*, a point the defendant had not proved.

Quilici v. Village of Morton Grove, 695 F.2d 261 (7th Cir. 1982), cert. denied, 464 U.S. 863 (1983). In rejecting a Second and Fourteenth Amendment challenge to a village handgun ban, the court held that the Second Amendment, either of itself or by incorporation through the Fourteenth Amendment, "does not apply to the states." The court, in dicta, commented on the "scope of the second amendment," summarizing *Miller* as holding that the right extends "only to those arms which are necessary to maintain a well regulated militia."

Thus, finding (without evidence) that "individually owned handguns [are not] military weapons," the court concluded that "the right to keep and bear handguns is not guaranteed by the second amendment."

***United States v. Nelson*, 859 F.2d 1318 (8th Cir. 1988).** This case involved the federal switchblade knife act. In a one-paragraph opinion, the Eighth Circuit misinterpreted *Cruikshank* as holding that the right to keep and bear arms is not fundamental. Without explanation, the Court cited *Miller*, *Oakes* and *Warin* as holding that the Second Amendment has been analyzed "purely in terms of protecting state militias, rather than individual rights."

***United States v. Emerson*, 270 F.3d 203 (5th Cir. 2001).** Defendant Emerson had been convicted of violating the federal law prohibiting possession of firearms by an individual under a certain kind of restraining order. The court found that the Second Amendment is not violated by "limited, narrowly tailored specific exceptions or restrictions for particular cases that are reasonable and not inconsistent with the right of Americans generally to individually keep and bear their private arms as historically understood in this country," noting that "felons, infants, and those of unsound mind may be prohibited from possessing firearms."

The court declared the right to arms to be an individually held right. The court said,

We have found no historical evidence that the Second Amendment was intended to convey militia power to

*the states ... or applies only to members of a select
militia.... All of the evidence indicates that the Second
Amendment, like other parts of the Bill of Rights,
applies to and protects individual Americans. We find
that the history of the Second Amendment reinforces
the plain meaning of its text, namely that it protects
individual Americans in their right to keep and bear
arms whether or not they are a member of a select militia
or performing active military service or training. We
reject the collective rights and sophisticated collective
rights models for interpreting the Second Amendment.
We hold, consistent with Miller, that it protects the
right of individuals, including those not then actually
a member of any militia or engaged in active military
service or training, to privately possess and bear their
own firearms....*

**Parker v. District of Columbia, 478 F.3d 370 (D.C.
Cir. 2007).** Plaintiffs challenged the District's laws
prohibiting handguns not already registered in the city, the
possession of an assembled, loaded firearm in one's home,
and use of any gun for defense against violent criminals
who invade a person's home. The court agreed with the
Supreme Court, the U.S. Court of Appeals for the Fifth
Circuit, the Justice Department, the Framers of the Bill of
Rights, and constitutional scholars past and present, that

*[T]he Second Amendment protects an individual
right to keep and bear arms. That right existed prior
to the formation of the new government under the
Constitution and was premised on the private use of
arms for activities such as hunting and self-defense,*

the latter being understood as resistance to either private lawlessness or the depredations of a tyrannical government (or a threat from abroad).

U.S. District Court Cases

***United States v. Gross*, 313 F.Supp. 1330 (S.D. Ind. 1970), aff'd on other grounds, 451 F.2d 1355 (7th Cir. 1971).** In rejecting a challenge to the constitutionality of the requirement that those who engage in the business of dealing in firearms must be licensed, the court, following its view of *Miller*, held that the defendant had not shown that "the licensing of dealers in firearms in any way destroys, or impairs the efficiency of, a well regulated militia."

***United States v. Kraase*, 340 F.Supp. 147 (E.D. Wis. 1972).** In ruling on a motion to dismiss an indictment, the court rejected a facial constitutional challenge to the federal law prohibiting sales of firearms by unlicensed individuals to residents of other states. Recognizing that an individual right was protected, it held that "second amendment protection might arise if proof were offered at the trial demonstrating that his possession of the weapon in question had a reasonable relationship to the maintenance of a 'well-regulated Militia.'"

***United States v. Bowdach*, 414 F.Supp. 1346 (D. S. Fla. 1976), aff'd, 561 F.2d 1160 (5th Cir. 1977).** The court held that "possession of [a] shotgun by a non-felon has no legal consequences. U.S. Const. Amend II."

United States v. Kozerski, **518 F.Supp. 1082 (D. N.H.1981), cert. denied, 469 U.S. 842 (1984).** In the context of a challenge to the law prohibiting the possession of firearms by convicted felons, the court, while holding correctly (see *Nelson*) that the Second Amendment "is not a grant of a right but a limitation upon the power of Congress and the national government," concluded that the right "is a collective right … rather than an individual right," citing only *Warin*. As a district court in the First Circuit, however, the court was bound by *Cases*, which expressly recognized that the right belonged to individuals.

Thompson v. Dereta, **549 F.Supp. 297 (D. Utah 1982).** An applicant for relief from disabilities (a prohibited person) brought an action against federal agents involved in denying his application. The court dismissed the case, holding that, because there was no "absolute constitutional right of an individual to possess a firearm," there was "no liberty or property interest sufficient to give rise to a procedural due process claim."

Vietnamese Fishermen's Assoc. v. KKK, **543 F.Supp. 198 (S.D. Tex. 1982).** Mischaracterizing *Miller*, the court held that the Second Amendment "prohibits only such infringement on the bearing of weapons as would interfere with the preservation or efficiency of 'a well regulated militia' organized by the State." Later, however, the court, following *Miller*, explained that the "Second Amendment's guarantee is limited to the right to keep and bear such arms as have 'a reasonable relationship to the preservation or efficiency of a well regulated militia.'" The court's understanding of the Second Amendment is, thus, inconsistent and, given the facts of the case, largely dicta.

Gilbert Equipment Co., Inc. v. Higgins, **709 F. Supp. 1071 (S.D. Ala. 1989), aff'd, 894 F.2d 412 (11th Cir. 1990).**   The court held that the Second Amendment "guarantees to all Americans 'the right to keep and bear arms.'"

APPENDIX C:
Suggested Reading On The Second Amendment

Law Reviews—Individual Right

Amar, Akhil R., The Bill of Rights as a Constitution, 100 Yale L.J. 1131, 1162-1175 (1991).

Barnett, Randy E., The Relevance of the Framers' Intent, 19 Harv. J. of L. & Pub. Pol'y 403-410 (1996).

_____, & Kates, Don B., Under Fire: The New Consensus on the Second Amendment, 45 Emory L.J. 1140-1259 (1996).

Bordenet, "The Right to Possess Arms: the Intent of the Framers of the Second Amendment", 21 U.W.L.A. L. Rev. 1 (1990).

Bursor, Scott "Toward a Functional Framework for Interpreting the Second Amendment," 74 Texas Law Review 1125-1151 (1996).

Cantrell, Charles L., The Right to Bear Arms: A Reply, 53 Wis. B. Bull. 21-26 (Oct. 1980).

Caplan, David I., The Right of the Individual to Bear Arms: A Recent Judicial Trend, 4 Det. L. Rev. 789-823 (1982).

_____, Restoring the Balance: The Second Amendment Revisited, 5 Fordham L.J. 31-53 (1976).

Chrisman, Christopher, Constitutional Structure and the Second Amendment: A Defense of the Individual Right to Keep and Bear Arms, 43 Ariz. L. Rev. 439 (2001).

Churchill, Robert H., "Gun Regulation, the Police Power, and the Right to Keep Arms in Early America: The Legal Context of the Second Amendment," 25 Law and History Review pages 139 to 176 (Spring 2007).

Comment, "Gun Control Legislation and the Intent of the Second Amendment: To What Extent is There an Individual Right to keep and Bear Arms?" 37 Villanova L. Rev. 1407 (1992).

Cottrol, Robert J., "Structure, Participation, Citizenship and Rights," 87 Georgetown L. J. 2307 (1999).

Cottrol, Robert J. and Raymond T. Diamond, "'The Fifth Auxiliary Right'", 104 Yale L. J. 995-1026 (1994).

_____, & Raymond T. Diamond, "'Never Intended to be Applied to the White Population': Firearms Regulation and Racial Disparity, The Redeemed South's Legacy to a National Jurisprudence?", 70 Chicago-Kent L. Rev. 1307 (1995).

Denning, Brannon P., "Gun Shy: The Second Amendment as an 'Underenforced Constitutional Norm'", 21 Har. J. L. & Pub. Pol'y 719 (1998).

_____, & Glenn Harlan Reynolds, "It Takes a Militia: A Communitarian Case for Compulsory Arms Bearing," 5 Wm. & M. Bill Of Rts. J. 185 (1997).

_____, "Palladium of Liberty? Cause and Consequences of the Federalization of State Militias in the Twentieth Century," 21 Okla. City U. L. Rev. 191 (1997).

_____,"Professional Discourse, The Second Amendment and the 'Talking Head Constitutionalism' Counterrevolution: A Review Essay," 21 SIU L. J. 227 (1997).

_____, "Can the Simple Cite Be Trusted: Lower Court Interpretations of United States v. Miller and the Second Amendment," 26 Cumberland L. Rev. 961-1004 (1996).

Dennis, Anthony, "Clearing the Smoke from the Right to Bear Arms and the Second Amendment," 29 Akron Law Review 57-92 (1995).

Dowlut, Robert, "The Right to Keep and Bear Arms: A Right to Self-Defense Against Criminals and Despots," 8 Stanford Law & Policy Rev. 25 (1997).

_____, "Bearing Arms in State Bills of Rights, Judicial Interpretation, and Public Housing," 5 St. Thomas L. Rev. 203 (1992).

_____, "Federal and State Constitutional Guarantees to Arms," 15 U. Dayton L. Rev. 59 (1989).

_____, "The Current Relevancy of Keeping and Bearing Arms," 15 U. Balt. L. For. 32 (1984).

_____, "The Right to Arms: Does the Constitution or the Predilection of Judges Reign?," 36 Oklahoma L. Rev. 65-105 (1983).

_____, & Janet A. Knoop, "State Constitutions and the Right to Keep and Bear Arms," 7 Okla. City U. L. Rev. 177-241 (1982).

Frye, Brian L., "The Peculiar Story of United States v. Miller," New York Univ. Journal of Law & Liberty (2007).

Funk, T. Markus, "Is the True Meaning of the Second Amendment Really Such A Riddle?," 39 Howard L. J. 411 (1995).

_____, "Gun Control and Economic Discrimination: The Melting-Point Case-in-Point", 85 J. Crim. L. & Criminol. 764, 776-789 (1995).

Gardiner, Richard E., "To Preserve Liberty—A Look at the Right to Keep and Bear Arms," 10 N. Ky. L. Rev. 63-96 (1982).

Gottlieb, Alan M., "Gun Ownership: A Constitutional Right," 10 N. Ky. L. Rev. 113-140 (1982).

Halbrook, Stephen P., "Second Class Citizenship and the Second Amendment in the District of Columbia," 5 GMU Civ. Rts. L.J. 105-178 (1995).

_____, "Personal Security, Personal Liberty, and 'The Constitutional Right to Bear Arms': Visions of the Framers of the Fourteenth Amendment," 5 Seton Hall Const. L.J. 341-434 (1995).

_____, "Congress Interprets the Second Amendment: Declarations by a Co-Equal Branch on the Individual Right to Keep and Bear Arms," 62 Tenn. L. Rev. 597-641 (1995).

_____, "What the Framers Intended: A Linguistic Interpretation of the Second Amendment," 49 Law & Contemp. Probs. 153 (1986).

_____, "Rationing Firearms Purchases and the Right to Keep Arms," 96 W. Va. L. Rev. 1 (1993).

_____, "The Right of the People or the Power of the State: Bearing Arms, Arming Militias, and the Second Amendment," 26 Valparaiso L. Rev. 131 (1991).

_____, "Encroachments of the Crown on the Liberty of the Subject: Pre-Revolutionary Origins of the Second Amendment," 15 U. Dayton L. Rev. 91 (1989).

_____, "To Keep and Bear Their Private Arms: The Adoption of the Second Amendment, 1787-1791," 10 N. Ky. L. Rev. 13-39 (1982).

_____, "The Jurisprudence of the Second and Fourteenth Amendments," 4 GMU L. Rev. 1-69 (1981).

Hardy, David T., "The Second Amendment and the Historiography of the Bill of Rights," 4 J. Law & Politics 1 (1987).

_____, "Armed Citizens, Citizen Armies: Toward a Jurisprudence of the Second Amendment," 9 Harv. J. Law & Pub. Pol'y 559 (1986).

Heath, J. Norman, "Exposing the Second Amendment: Federal Preemption of State Militia Legislation," 79 U. Det. Mercy L. Rev.39 (2001).

Johnson, Nicholas J., "The Intersection of Abortion and Gun Rights," 50 Rutgers L. Rev. 97 (1997).

_____, "Plenary Power and Constitutional Outcasts: Federal Power, Critical Race Theory and the Second, Ninth and Tenth Amendments," 57 Ohio St. L. J. 1556 (1996).

_____, "Shots Across No Man's Land: A Response to Handgun Control, Inc.'s Richard Aborn," 22 Fordham Urban L. J. 441-451 (1995).

Kates, Don B. Jr., "Gun Control: Separating Reality from Symbolism," 20 J. Contemp. L. 353-379 (1994).

_____, "The Second Amendment and the Ideology of Self-Protection," 9 Const. Comm. 87-104 (1992).

_____, "The Second Amendment: A Dialogue," 49 L. & Contemp. Probs. 143-150 (1986).

_____, "Handgun Prohibition and the Original Meaning of the Second Amendment," 82 Mich. L. Rev. 204-273 (1983).

Kopel, David B., "The Second Amendment in the Nineteenth Century," 1998 Brig. Young L. Rev. 1359.

_____, & Christopher Little, "Communitarians, Neo-Republicans, and Guns: Assessing the Case for Firearms Prohibition," Maryland L. Rev. # 2 (1997).

_____, & Joseph Olson, "Preventing a Reign of Terror: Civil Liberties Implications of Terrorism Legislation," 21 Okla. City U. L. Rev. 247 (1997).

_____, "It Isn't About Duck Hunting: The British Origins of the Right to Arms," 93 Mich. L. Rev. 1333 (1995).

Larish, Inge Anna, "Why Annie Can't Get a Gun: A Feminist Appraisal of the 2nd Am.," 1996 U. Ill. Law F. 467.

Levinson, Sanford, "The Embarrassing Second Amendment," 99 Yale L.J. 637-659 (1989).

Lund, Nelson, "The End of Second Amendment Jurisprudence: Firearms Disabilities and Domestic Violence Restraining Orders," 4 Tex. Rev. L & Politics 181 (1999).

_____, "The Past and Future of the Individual's Right to Arms," 31 Georgia Law Review 1 (1996).

_____, "The Second Amendment, Political Liberty and the Right to Self-Preservation", 39 Ala. L. Rev. 103 (1987).

Malcolm, Joyce Lee, "The Right of the People to Keep and Bear Arms: The Common Law Tradition," 10 Hast. Const. L. Q. 285 (1983).

Martire, "In Defense of the Second Amendment: Constitutional and Historical Perspectives," 21 Linc. L. Rev. 23 (1993).

Massey, Calvin, "Guns, Extremists and the Constitution," 57 Wash. & Lee L. Rev. 1095 (2000).

McAffee, Thomas, "Constitutional Limits on Regulating Private Militia Groups," 58 Mont. L. Rev. 45 (1997).

_____, & Michael J. Quinlan, "Bringing Forward The Right to Keep and Bear Arms: Do Text, History or Precedent Stand in the Way?," 75 U. N.C. L. Rev. 781 (1997).

Moncure, Thomas, "The Second Amendment Ain't About Hunting," 34 How. L. J. 589 (1991).

_____, "Who is the Militia - The Virginia Ratifying Convention and the Right to Bear Arms," 19 Linc. L. Rev. 1 (1990).

Morgan, Eric C., "Assault Rifle Legislation: Unwise and Unconstitutional," 17 Am. J. Crim. L. 143 (1990).

O'Hare, Robert A. and Jorge Pedreira, "An Uncertain Right: The Second Amendment and the Assault Weapon Legislation Controversy," 66 St. John's L. Rev. 179 (1992).

Powe, Jr., L. A. Scot, "Guns, Words and Constitutional Interpretation," 38 Wm. & M. L. Rev. 1311-1403 (1997).

Quinlan, Michael J., "Is There a Neutral Justification for Refusing to Implement the Second Amendment or is the Supreme Court Just 'Gun Shy,'" 22 Capital U. L. Rev. 641 (1995).

Rabkin, Jeremy, "Constitutional Firepower: New Light on the Meaning of the Second Amendment," 86 J. Crim. L. & Criminol. 231-246 (1995).

Reynolds, Glenn H., "A Critical Guide to the Second Amendment," 62 Tenn. L. Rev. 461-512 (1995).

_____, "The Right to Keep and Bear Arms Under the Tennessee Constitution", 61 Tenn. L. Rev. 647 (1994).

Richards, Haydn J., Jr., Redefining the Second Amendment: The Antebellum Right to Keep and Bear Arms and Its Present Legacy," 91 Ky. L.J. 311-351 (2002).

Roots, Roger, "The Approaching Death of the Collective Right Theory of the Second Amendment," 39 Duq. L. Rev. 71, 88ff. (2000).

Shalhope, Robert, "The Armed Citizen in the Early Republic," 49 Law & Contemp. Probs. 125 (1986).

_____, "The Ideological Origins of the Second Amendment, 69 J. of Am. Hist. 599 (1982).

Shelton, Gregory Lee, "In Search of the Lost Amendment: Challenging Federal Firearms Regulation Through Utilization of the State's Right Interpretation of the Second Amendment," 23 Florida State U. L. Rev. 105 (1995).

Szezepanski, Kevin D., "Searching for the Plain Meaning of the Second Amendment," 44 Buff. L. Rev. 197 (1996).

Tahmassebi, Stefan, "Gun Control and Racism," 2 Geo. Mason Civ. Rts. L. J. 67 (1991).

Van Alstyne, William, "The Second Amendment and the Personal Right to Arms," 43 Duke L. J. 1236-1255 (1994).

Vandercoy, David, "The History of the Second Amendment," 28 Valparaiso L. Rev. 1006 (1994).

Volokh, Eugene, "The Commonplace Second Amendment," 73 N.Y.U. L. Rev. 793 (1998).

_____, "The Amazing Vanishing Second Amendment," 73 N.Y.U. L. Rev. 831.

Walker, William A., Review, 88 Mich. L. Rev. 1409-14 (1990).

Wayment, Andrew M., "The Second Amendment: A Guard for Our Future Security," 37 Idaho L. Rev. 203 (2000).

Worthen, Kevin, "The Right to Keep and Bear Arms in Light of Thornton: The People and Essential Attributes of Sovereignty," 1998 Brig. Young L. Rev. 137.

Law Reviews—Collective Right

Bellesiles, Michael A., "Suicide Pact: New Readings of the Second Amendment," 16 Const. Comment. 247, 256 (1999).

————, "The Second Amendment in Action," 76 Chicago-Kent L. Rev. 61 (2000).

Blodgett-Ford, Sayoko, "Do Battered Women Have a Right to Bear Arms?," 11 Yale L. & Pol. Rev. 509-560 (1993).

Bogus, Carl T., "The History and Politics of Second Amendment Scholarship: A Primer," 76 Chicago-Kent L. Rev. 3 (2000).

Dorf, Michael C., "What Does the Second Amendment Mean Today?," 76 Chicago-Kent L. Rev. 291 (2000).

Ehrman, Keith A. & Henigan, Dennis A., "The Second Amendment in the Twentieth Century: Have You Seen Your Militia Lately?," 15 U. Dayton L. Rev. 5 (1989).

Daniel A. Farber, "Disarmed by Time: The Second Amendment and the Failure of Originalism," 76 Chicago-Kent L. Rev. 167 (2000).

Fields, Samuel, "Guns, Crime and the Negligent Gun Owner," 10 N. Ky. L.R. (1982)

Finkelman, Paul, "'A Well Regulated Militia': The Second Amendment in Historical Perspective," 76 Chicago-Kent L. Rev. 195 (2000).

Henigan, Dennis A., "Arms, Anarchy and the Second Amendment," 26 Val. U. L. Rev. 107 (1991).

Heyman, Steven J., "Natural Rights and the Second Amendment," 76 Chicago-Kent L. Rev. 237 (2000).

Rakove, Jack N., "The Second Amendment: The Highest Stage of Originalism," 76 Chicago-Kent L. Rev. 103 (2000).

Schwoerer, Lois G., "To Hold and Bear Arms: The English Perspective," 76 Chicago-Kent L. Rev. 27 (2000).

Spannaus, "State Firearms Regulation and the Second Amendment," 6 Hamline L.R. 383 (1983).

Spitzer, Robert J., "Lost and Found: Researching the Second Amendment," 76 Chicago-Kent L. Rev. 349 (2000).

Uviller, H. Richard & William G. Merkel, "The Second Amendment in Context: The Case of the Vanishing Predicate," 76 Chicago-Kent L. Rev. 403 (2000).

Williams, David C., "The Unitary Second Amendment," 73 N.Y.U. L. Rev. 822-830 (1998).

_____, "Civic Republicanism and the Citizen Militia: The Terrifying Second Amendment," 101 Yale L.J. 551, 586–94 (1991).

_____, "The Militia Movement and Second Amendment Revolution: Conjuring with the People," 81 Cornell L. Rev. 879 (1996).

Winkler, Adam, "Scrutinizing the Second Amendment," 105 Mich. L. Rev. 683 (2007).

_____, "The Reasonable Right to Bear Arms," 17 Stanford Law & Policy Review 597 (2006).

Yassky, David, "The Second Amendment: Structure, History, and Constitutional Change," 99 Mich. L. Rev. 588, 615–21 (2000).

156

APPENDIX D:
The Founders on the Second Amendment

Thomas Jefferson, of Virginia:

"The constitutions of most of our States assert that all power is inherent in the people; that ... it is their right and duty to be at all times armed."

-Letter to John Cartwright, 1824

"Laws that forbid the carrying of arms. . . disarm only those who are neither inclined nor determined to commit crimes. . . Such laws make things worse for the assaulted and better for the assailants; they serve rather to encourage than to prevent homicides, for an unarmed man may be attacked with greater confidence than an armed man."

-Jefferson's "Commonplace Book," 1774-1776,
quoting from *On Crimes and Punishment,*
by criminologist Cesare Beccaria, 1764

George Mason, of Virginia:

"[W]hen the resolution of enslaving America was formed in Great Britain, the British Parliament was advised by an artful man, who was governor of Pennsylvania, to disarm the people; that it was the best and most effectual way to enslave them; but that they should not do it openly, but weaken them, and let them sink gradually."

"[I] ask, who are the militia? They consist now of the whole people, except a few public officers."
-Virginia's U.S. Constitution ratification convention, 1788

"That the People have a right to keep and bear Arms; that a well regulated Militia, composed of the Body of the People, trained to arms, is the proper, natural, and safe Defence of a free state."
> -Within Mason's declaration of "the essential and unalienable Rights of the People,"—later adopted by the Virginia ratification convention, 1788

Samuel Adams, of Massachusetts:

"The said Constitution [shall] be never construed to authorize Congress to infringe the just liberty of the press, or the rights of conscience; or to prevent the people of the United States, who are peaceable citizens, from keeping their own arms."
> -Massachusetts' U.S. Constitution ratification convention, 1788

William Grayson, of Virginia:

"[A] string of amendments were presented to the lower House; these altogether respected personal liberty."
> -Letter to Patrick Henry, June 12, 1789, referring to the introduction of what became the Bill of Rights

Richard Henry Lee, of Virginia:

"A militia when properly formed are in fact the people themselves . . . and include all men capable of bearing arms. . . To preserve liberty it is essential that the whole body of people always possess arms... The mind that aims at a select militia, must be influenced by a truly anti-republican principle."
          -Additional Letters From The Federal Farmer, 1788

James Madison, of Virginia:

The Constitution preserves "the advantage of being armed which Americans possess over the people of almost every other nation. . . (where) the governments are afraid to trust the people with arms."
                                        -The Federalist, No. 46

Tench Coxe, of Pennsylvania:

"The militia, who are in fact the effective part of the people at large, will render many troops quite unnecessary. They will form a powerful check upon the regular troops, and will generally be sufficient to over-awe them."
                              -An American Citizen, Oct. 21, 1787

"Who are the militia? Are they not ourselves? Congress have no power to disarm the militia. Their swords and every other terrible implement of the soldier, are the birthright of an American . . . . The unlimited power of the sword is not in the hands of either the federal or state governments, but, where I trust in God it will ever remain,

in the hands of the people."
> *-The Pennsylvania Gazette*, Feb. 20, 1788

"As the military forces which must occasionally be raised to defend our country, might pervert their power to the injury of their fellow citizens, the people are confirmed by the next article (of amendment) in their right to keep and bear their private arms."
> *-Federal Gazette*, June 18, 1789

Noah Webster, of Pennsylvania:

"Before a standing army can rule, the people must be disarmed; as they are in almost every kingdom in Europe. The supreme power in America cannot enforce unjust laws by the sword; because the whole body of the people are armed, and constitute a force superior to any band of regular troops that can be, on any pretence, raised in the United States. A military force, at the command of Congress, can execute no laws, but such as the people perceive to be just and constitutional; for they will possess the power."
> *-An Examination of The Leading Principles of the Federal Constitution*, 1787

Alexander Hamilton, of New York:

"[I]f circumstances should at any time oblige the government to form an army of any magnitude, that army can never be formidable to the liberties of the people while there is a large body of citizens, little if at all inferior to them in discipline and the use of arms, who stand ready to

defend their rights and those of their fellow citizens."
-The Federalist, No. 29

Thomas Paine, of Pennsylvania:

"[A]rms discourage and keep the invader and plunderer in awe, and preserve order in the world as well as property.... Horrid mischief would ensue were the law-abiding deprived of the use of them."
-Thoughts On Defensive War, 1775

Fisher Ames, of Massachusetts:

"The rights of conscience, of bearing arms, of changing the government, are declared to be inherent in the people."
-Letter to F.R. Minoe, June 12, 1789

Elbridge Gerry, of Massachusetts:

"What, sir, is the use of militia? It is to prevent the establishment of a standing army, the bane of liberty. . . Whenever Government means to invade the rights and liberties of the people, they always attempt to destroy the militia, in order to raise a standing army upon its ruins."
-Debate, U.S. House of Representatives, August 17, 1789

Patrick Henry, of Virginia:

"Guard with jealous attention the public liberty. Suspect everyone who approaches that jewel."
-Virginia's U.S. Constitution ratification convention